It has been said,

a book is a better monument

than stone.

Cover:

Chaplain Allen Allensworth about the time of his retirement from the Army

Out of Darkness, The Story of Allen Allensworth

© 1995

Published by Inkling Press 1998

PO Box 2598

Menlo Park, California 94026

OUT OF DARKNESS

THE STORY OF ALLEN ALLENSWORTH

BY

EVELYN RADCLIFFE

Chaplain Allensworth at one of the duty stations to which he was assigned

Preface

Lieutenant Colonel Allen Allensworth is one of the unsung heroes of Afro-American culture. His story needs to be known. He inspired great numbers to gain an education. His excellent services to his country and his exemplary moral character presented a role model for Army and Navy personnel. His allegiance to the highest Christian principles and his accomplishments in the face of trials make him an outstanding contribution to Afro-American history.

He was born into slavery but with a gift from divine Providence that would lead him to the top of his profession in many walks of life: *the deep, sincere and burning desire for learning.* At a very young age he heard from his wise mother the promise that education could offer. She made him see that without the advantage of an education a man can never hope for success in the important things of life.

He never stopped learning, seeking, reading and filling his mind with knowledge. Because of this he became a good slave, a kindly army nurse, a fine soldier, restaurateur, Army Officer, Preacher, Teacher, Lecturer, Chaplain, husband, father and town founder. He submerged all the color prejudices that would accompany such an upward path. Through perseverance, love of the Bible, and keeping his eye on the promise he escaped the darkness in which the nature of birth would have encased him.

I became interested in this man after seeing a short documentary, dealing mainly with the town of Allensworth. I literally fell in love with his picture in his Chaplain's uniform and began a search for information about him. There was very little to be found. I couldn't believe that so honorable a man of achievement could have disappeared into the past with so little esteem. I searched throughout many libraries in California, including the prestigious Bancroft Library at the University of California, Berkeley. I researched his Army and Navy records, the history of Kentucky, the State of California records, Civil War reports, The Spanish American War, Afro American history, the National Archives, the Bettman Archives and so on and on. I thoroughly enjoyed every minute of it. Finding so little of his accomplishments recorded, however, I decided I must do something about it. I could write pages of the strange little happy coincidences that aided my search, showing that a hand greater than mine was on this project.

Catherine Drinker Bowen, the well-known biographer, says a writer of biographies must feel of his subject that he simply "cannot bear that this man should be forgotten or exist only in dry eulogy or brief paragraphs in history textbooks."[1] These words are the cause of this biography.

CHAPTER 1

The small slave boy stood by the roadside and watched the plantation owner's children come home from school.

What he saw under their arms called up the utmost yearning, a desire that haunted him constantly. They had BOOKS! How he ached to learn to read. Somehow he knew that the hieroglyphics in those books spelled information that would guide him to freedom. He hungered for books of his own. The only things that belonged to him were the clothes on his back, which his mother tried hard to keep clean and well patched. In those pre-Civil War days only white children were allowed to go to school. Because of his color little Allen was not. It was illegal for children of slaves even to teach *themselves* to read.

Allen was born in a crude slave shack on the plantation of A.P. Starbird, in Louisville, Kentucky. On April 7, 1842, Phyllis and Levi welcomed this child, their thirteenth. Phyllis chose the name of Allen after a well-known African Methodist Episcopal Church leader. There are no records to ascertain that she and Levi ever married, so it is believed that the "Allensworth" name was just assumed because of Phyllis' admiration for Bishop Allen. (See end of chapter.)

Little Allen grew as steadily as the rows of cotton in back of their shack. Before he was old enough, or tall enough to be seen among the rows his chores began. His entire days bulged with work around the plantation. Soon, owner, A.P. Starbird and his wife Bett gave the little slave to Tommy, their son. This was the custom in those days. From then on Allen was Tommy's "boy," and Tommy was the "Marse" (master) in all their doings.

The hymn-singing Phyllis, had a gentleness and obedience that made her a favorite of her owners. Her influence on her small son taught him the value of integrity and honesty. She let him know she wanted freedom and the good things of life for him.

"To be a great and good man, and a useful man to others, you must know how to read the Bible and fit yourself to live up to its teachings", she often told him.

One summer evening Phyllis and Allen enjoyed a few rare moments of rest together on the slanting porch of their cabin. The occasional toot-toot of an excursion boat, steaming down the Ohio River nearby, added melody to the shadowy twilight. The plump lady, in her faded green calico dress, with her early graying head wrapped in a white kerchief knotted at the corners, spoke to the boy.

"My son, Miss Bett is sending 'Little Marse' Tommy to school, to get a learnin'; now, my son," she said, "what is good for 'Little Marse' is good for you. Your mother can't send you to no school where you can learn to read and write and figure, so you must ask your "Marse" Tom to play school with you every day when he comes home; then you can learn to read and write like him, only don't let on to him that I told you to do it".

To most slaves even the very *words* 'reading' and 'writing' were mysterious and dangerous. One young slave said, "We get whupt bad if they ketch us with even a paper of writing in our hands."

A slave from Louisiana, a midwife and nurse explained the situation: "I wanted to git the papers for midwifing, but lawsy, I don't never have no time for larnin in slave time. If Marse kotch a paper in you hand he sure whup you. He don't 'low no bright niggers round, he sell 'em quick. He always say, 'Book larnin don't raise no good sugar cane.' The only larnin he 'low was when they larn the colored children the Methodist catechism. The only writin' a nigger ever git am when he git born or marry or die, then Marse put the name in the big book."[2]

Phyllis instinctively knew in her heart that if a child as bright as Allen received only a partial education he could win his freedom from the limitations of a life of slavery. She reminded her son of Bishop Allen's example, and her hopes that he would grow up to be like the respected church leader. It is clear that he never forgot his mother's words. But later years would show that Levi's commendable honesty and careful use of money also left their mark on Allen .

While his son, Allen, was still a very small child, Levi took his courage in his hands and asked his master for their freedom. The two men entered into an agreement in which Levi could buy his freedom for twelve hundred dollars. This was to be paid in three payments of four hundred dollars each. With the debt paid off, Levi would receive his free papers. This practice was called manumitting.

By procuring two mules and a cart, Levi transported crops from Louisville about eighty miles south to Portland, Kentucky. Levi had managed to make his first two payments, when one day, totally unexpectedly, he found he had been sold to another master. When Levi explained to his new owner, a Mr. Colliers, it turned out the reason for the transfer was to pay a large debt owed to Colliers.

Already crushed and shocked, Levi then learned that his payments would go on in the same deal with the new owner, but at twice the rate! He had held high hopes of buying Phyllis' freedom after his own. Now his plans were shattered. Heart broken and bowed down with disappointment and many more strenuous chores, Levi became ill and soon died.

The loss of his father left Allen, not yet eight years old, in a pit of deep, dark grief. But Phyllis' sorrow was deeper. Despondency and depression shrouded her thought and work for months. It so displeased Miss Bett, the owner's wife, that she had the meek slave sold to an owner three plantations away from the Starbirds. Phyllis had the reputation among neighboring plantation-owners as a fine cook especially noted for her delicious pastry, so it wasn't hard to find a buyer for her.

At her new farm, owned by attorney Nat Wolfe, were Wolfe's two sons, Willie and Nat, Jr. Allen and "Marse" Tommy sometimes went down the road to his mother's place to play with Nat and Willie. Allen was the only black in the foursome and consequently looked on as somewhat inferior. The boys had mock battles with other children in the neighborhood and Allen always bore the brunt of their games. One day as they were enjoying a good bout, one of the Wolfe boys threw a heavy stone hitting Allen over his left eye, resulting in a scar he carried throughout his life. Retribution does soften some of life's blows, however, as Allen was to find some 35 years later.

•　　　•　　　•

Even in his mother's absence, Allen and Tommy, kept up their secret school days in an upper room in the Starboard's large house. On one rainy afternoon, Miss Bett Starbird burst in upon them and discovered the boys with their books. Her eyes flashed with anger that appeared to promise punishment.

"If I ever catch you doing this again I'll thrash your hide" she told them.

After the third time they were caught, red handed, Miss Bett decided the only solution was to find another home for Allen. A retail merchant, Mr. Talbot needed a young boy to do odd jobs around the house to help his mother. So Allen, at the age of twelve, moved to a new household that would give him the closest hint of happiness he had known yet.

Slave children working in the sugar cane fields 1852.

$1200

TO

1250 DOLLARS !

FOR NEGROES !!

THE undersigned wishes to purchase a large lot of NEGROES for the New Orleans market. I will pay $1200 to $1250 for No. 1 young men, and $850 to $1000 for No. 1 young women. In fact I will pay more for likely

NEGROES,

Than any other trader in Kentucky. My office is adjoining the Broadway Hotel, on Broadway, Lexington, Ky., where I or my Agent can always be found.

WM. F. TALBOTT.

LEXINGTON, JULY 2, 1853.

Advertisement for slaves in the South. The "Talbott" may have been at one time the owner of Allensworth, despite the difference in spelling.

CHAPTER 2

Mrs. Talbot, a Quaker lady, had high principles, deep love for everyone and a very religious sense. She let Allen sleep on a neat cot in her own bedroom. She taught him the familiar children's prayer,

> "Now I lay me down to sleep;
> I pray the Lord my soul to keep.
> If I should die before I wake,
> I pray the Lord my soul to take".

She said it with him every night. And she actually helped him with his lessons.

The warm-hearted lady even took the young boy to town and bought him a suit to replace the worn, tattered and patched overalls he had. Real, store-bought clothes! The reassuring feel of being neatly clad in fine clothing remained with Allen throughout his life. In later years his friends knew him as "one of the neatest men of the Negro race."

One Sunday, when he happened to be dressed in his new suit his mother visited him on the Talbot's plantation. She was so pleased to see him looking prosperous her eyes welled with tears of joy and she said, over and over, "Thankie Jesus, Thankie Jesus." She firmly believed and acknowledged that everything good came from God.

Compared with earlier days, life with the Talbots seemed close to heaven for Allen, despite all the hard work he must do. Mrs. Talbot spent time giving him secret lessons in reading and writing. And soon her Church started a Sunday school for the children of slaves. Among the first lessons they were taught was "Servants obey your masters". Then came the Lord's Prayer and the Ten Commandments.

Allen's deep-seated desire to learn made him an apt pupil and under Mrs. Talbot's tutelage he advanced rapidly. He was learning! Then, one day nosey Miss Bett, back on the Starbirds' farm, heard through neighborhood gossip, about his rapid progress and was utterly dismayed. She felt this learning was injurious to the boy's future; Mrs. Talbot would ruin him for life. She felt that the "development of his mind would implant in his heart a discontent and a spirit of unrest that would completely un-fit him for the performance of his duties as a slave."

Something must be done at once!

The Starbirds' partner in business, John Smith, owned a plantation run by his brother Pat Smith, in Henderson County, Kentucky, about a hundred miles west of Louisville. Bett Starbird heard that Pat Smith needed a young slave. She willfully maneuvered Allen's transfer. So it was, that one day Mrs. Talbot called to Allen.

"My boy, Miss Bett has found a new home for you", she told him. "Gather your clothes together and bring them here."

A new home? What a crushing blow this was to Allen. A reluctant Mrs. Talbot and her husband, with Bett's help, arranged for Allen to meet John Smith on board the boat that would carry them to their destination.

Fear and uncertainty chased themselves around in Allen's mind concerning the move to another plantation. He realized how much he had enjoyed the wide, rolling meadows of bluegrass and the heavily wooded banks of the curving Ohio river nearby. Not to mention the friendly atmosphere on the Talbot's farm. And he had done nothing wrong. It seemed a punishment too severe for one whose only crime was trying to learn more.

To slaves in those days this action was called being "sold down the river", and Allen knew what it meant. The phrase seemed to indicate the most dreadful thing a slave could think of next to lashes with a cat-o'-nine-tails. It generally meant going to a slave master probably more cruel than the last. To Allen it meant an even harsher sentence, being so far away from his mother.

As he prepared to leave, Mrs. Talbot summoned her driver, "uncle" Rueben. (In that part of the South in Allen's day, people generally called their favored and gentler slaves "uncle" or "aunt" so-and-so). The thoughtful Mrs. Talbot gave Rueben orders to stop by Allen's mother's house so he could say goodbye. In another touching gesture of kindness Mrs. Talbot handed him a neat little knapsack in which she had tied up all his belongings. It included his new suit, a knife and his little blanket; more possessions than he had ever called his own. For a fleeting moment he felt a swelling pride of ownership, and manliness that puffed up his spirit like the pouter pigeons he'd seen in back of the Talbot's mansion. But the elation soon evaporated for the young slave.

His mother's house was only ten squares away from the Talbots but it had been months since he had the freedom to go there. Uncle Rueben knocked at the door.

"Come in" the husky voice called weakly.

What a sad and shocking scene greeted Allen on entering the house! Instead of the robust mother in his memory, he saw an aging, fragile little body, still wearing her usual gray calico dress. Pain grasped Allen's heart as he looked on the feeble figure. He saw his beloved mother, who had already lost twelve of her children to slavery, and her last-born was being sold down the river. He could almost see her withered hopes as despair shattered her chances for the companionship she would need in her waning years. She realized the separation was the result of one woman's foolish opinions. Even old Rueben tried to blink away the stinging in his eyes.

Frail and trembling, Phyllis forced herself up off the bed. She went to a small cupboard and pulled out a silver half dollar.

"Take this my son", she said when she could speak through her tears. "Buy yourself a book and a comb. Put knowledge from the book into your head, and comb everything else out with the comb".[3]

So with her last hope, she gave her last coin to her last child and turned to the wall feeling this was the end of everything good.

CHAPTER 3

Within an hour of that heart breaking scene Allen found himself on the way to the docks. headed apprehensively for his next adventure. Behind him lay the harmony of friendly, helpful owners and a touch of self-worth he had never known. Was that feeling gone forever, he wondered, or was it a promising foretaste of what the future might unfold to him?

Rueben's cart jiggled along slowly. Was it a coincidence that they happened to pass the only bookstore in town?

"Stop the cart!" Allen shouted.

The old man kindly stopped so Allen could, in his in-born obedience to his mother, buy the very first book the twelve-year old would call his own.

He knew exactly he wanted. He bought the book that all slaves with a desire to learn aspired to owning. Webster's Spelling Book, a small blue black dictionary type volume spelled a degree of freedom to his people. Numbers of them knew that education was their promise of escape, and this little book the major key.

Wise old Uncle Rueben took the treasure from Allen's hands and pointed to the picture on the frontispiece. It showed a woman, holding a child by the hand, leading him into a building. Rueben explained that the woman symbolized Allen's mother. The child she held by the hand was Allen. The building to which the mother pointed with her other hand signified the "temple of knowledge." In the slow and dusky dialect common at that time, Rueben explained the symbolism to young Allen.

"Knowledge is the greatest power in the world and the man

who possesses it and uses it in the wisest and best way can become a famous man."

"The devil," he continued, "will try to keep you from the temple of larnin; but don't you let him do it. Your ma wants you famous and you kin do it. Don't let nothin get in your way."

When Allen boarded the stern-wheeler *Rainbow* Uncle Rueben went on board with him. The river-boat scudded out into the Ohio River on a warm spring day in 1854. Allen and Uncle Rueben quickly met up with John Smith as arranged by Mrs. Talbot. Like that sympathetic lady, John Smith, a warm-hearted, fatherly man, took a liking to the young slave. He was on his way to Henderson County to visit his brother Pat. John saw to it that Allen did not get put in chains and huddled with the other slaves on the boat's hot and smelly lower deck.

Smith, instead, introduced him to uncle Dabney, a colored steward who had served on board the *Rainbow* for most of his life. Dabney was held in esteem in the thoughts of all who ever traveled on the boat, a man of distinction to both white and coloreds. Allen found out that uncle Dabney belonged to his mother's church in Louisville and that gave them a strong bond of friendship.

Uncle Dabney furnished Allen generously with food for thought as well as his body. He taught him to look for and enjoy the beauty as the boat slid along the lush and verdant river banks. He aroused in Allen a desire to become a steward. Stewards and cabin boys, Allen noticed, always looked spruced up and clean in their white jackets and aprons.

The slaves chained on the lower deck ate only corn meal mush, served in a trough, animal-style, but cabin boys could have whatever they could scrounge of the fancy food passengers left on their plates. Sometimes Allen could hear the adult slaves below singing mournful, pathetic sorrow-songs. Amid their grief these deeply religious, long suffering folks wailed and moaned their appeal to God for deliverance. By contrast, in Allen's eyes the cabin boys presented an example of the life refined and educated people lived.

He watched very carefully the manner in which they waited on tables to learn all he could. To become a cabin boy or steward became the hope that urged him to do rightly. As a first step in that direction, Uncle Dabney generously gave him a table to wait on. Here he learned a skill that would fit him for a higher class of slavery than the menial tasks that had collared him before.

Allen learned a lot observing life on the *Rainbow;* both good and bad; life such as he had never experienced before. True, he had seen his share of beatings, and human suffering due to sheer hatred. On the ship, however he witnessed brutal stabbings and shootings, resulting from gambling, lust and drunkenness. It shocked and astounded him to see these things among the "respected" white folks.

His work as cabin boy made the time speed by like the foam in the ship's wake and soon they churned into the Henderson harbor. His heart thumped extra hard as he pondered what lay ahead for him.

No Schoolin'

CHAPTER 4

On land once again Allen enjoyed the trip with John Smith to his brother Pat Smith's plantation. The three mile donkey ride from where the *Rainbow* docked in Henderson gave Allen a chance to rest and think before his duties began. As the donkey plodded its rickety cart, and passengers Smith and his charge, down the road, Allen remembered how uncle Dabney who had now gone back home, showed him how to appreciate the beauty around him. He admired the soft green moss hanging from giant oak and hickory trees. The crazy freedom of squirrels scampering among the cottonwood trees amused him. He noticed the familiar orderliness of cultivated fields. The soft sound of cooing doves played against the scritch scritch of the cart's wheels. With the fragrance of oleanders permeating the air, the whole scene made him shiver in anticipation of life on the Pat Smith plantation.

Allen's first friends in the Smith household were Eddie, an orphaned white boy, aunt Betty the cook, and aunt Phyllis the housekeeper. He quickly became fond of the housekeeper, since she had the same name as his mother. Mr. and Mrs. Smith instructed him to call them "Marse Pat" and "Miss Hebe".

At this early age, Allen showed signs of becoming an astute, discerning lad, eagerly aware of all manner of possibilities that seemed just out of his reach. When given the choice of which corner he would sleep in, he took his one little blanket and wisely chose the dining room. Here he could be close to the smell of food. In this spot, too he would be near enough to his master's room to answer quickly when they called during the night. Marse Pat gave him a small box in which to keep his belongings.

One day Miss Hebe, opened the box and found the comb Allen had bought with the money his mother had given him. Miss Hebe decided the comb was much too lovely for him and took it for herself. In its place she gave him a wool carder, an implement like a wire brush used to comb wool fibers to prepare them for spinning and weaving. She no doubt thought this would work better on his woolly head. Thus began a string of injustices the boy would suffer from the Smiths. (In his adulthood, Allen would relate others to his biographer.)

"One of the most torturing whippings I ever received," he told a writer, "was from Pat Smith and his brother Bob, when I was charged with purloining a bank note. I had been sent to town on an errand, and returning with this bank bill, gave it to Miss Hebe while she was reading. She placed it between the leaves of the book she was reading, continued to read and turn the leaves. Closing the book and laying it aside, she forgot what became of the bank note, and charged me with stealing it. I was denuded, tied, bucked and gagged, and for three hours I was whipped unmercifully. This castigation was to force me to confess to the purloining of the bank note.

"The torture was so great and the pain so intense that I finally confessed that I took the money, thinking that they would cease beating me; but then I could not tell what I did with it. I told all sorts of stories when they demanded to know what I did with it and none of them was true. Yet they continued to ply the leather lash to my lacerated body. I could not cry out. I could only moan and groan. They finally released me.

"Two days afterwards Miss Hebe took up the book to continue the story." [It could possibly have been the engrossing *Uncle*

Tom's Cabin, whose appearance had just caused a sensation among plantation owners.] "She found the bill. I was simply informed that they had found the bill where she had placed it, but, of course nothing was done as a redress for the horrible treatment I had received, nor to relieve my injured feeling."[4]

To those who witnessed slaves being lynched merely on a white owner's accusation, without anything as civilized as a trial, Allen's lashing might seem mild punishment. Even in the atmosphere of such cruelty, Allen decided to try to do everything right on the Smith plantation, to do his duty, to be truthful, obedient and industrious. This attitude contrasted sharply with that of many of the slaves of the period. Few of them ever had the joy of a reward for doing right. They seldom had any reason to do well except to avoid whippings. An earned reward furthers ambition but how would they learn about that? So disciplined by slavery, they survived by humble, self-effacing servitude to their masters, not aspiring for anything better. Slavery was their lot. In a kiss-the-hand-that-beats-you attitude some even came to love their owners, and lived in resigned bondage.

And then there was Allen Allensworth. He would never be content to be someone else's person. He had a deep, abiding desire for betterment under whatever circumstances he found himself. This grew into his life-long philosophy. Always he aimed for something higher, better, more progressive than the last.

Allen tolerated his experience on the Smith plantation, despite the constant burden of hard work and possible injustices always hovering over him. When he arrived that spring he owned only summer clothes. By the time the chill of fall and winter came his clothes were tattered and worn out. He was used to going barefoot in the summer, but frost on the ground became another matter. His feet, cracked and often bleeding caused him much pain.

One chilling fall day he asked Miss Hebe (Mrs. Smith) about a pair of shoes.

"Probably at Christmas time you'll receive a new pair," she said.

In the meantime he had to tread the frigid, crusty ground in the fields early every morning when he gathered the corn to feed the animals. Once he discovered that he could wrap his feet in the corn husks for a little comfort. At the coldest times, he found a little comfort by chasing the cows and pigs from their stalls and standing in the warmth of their beds until his feet were warm enough to walk back to the corn fields.

On occasions when they did acquire new shoes, some of the slaves would walk to Church on Sunday in their bare feet, carrying their shoes until they neared the church. They would dust off their feet, put on the shoes and strut proudly, hoping they looked like plantation owner's children.

The friendship between Allen and Eddie, the white orphan, flourished like the sorghum stalks they tended. It seemed odd to both of them that Eddie, could go to school, and got whipped for *not* getting his lessons. The boys had fun together on occasion, but Allen's really closest companion remained his little spelling book. When Mrs. Smith discovered Allen's devotion to it she, as the others before her, demanded that he stop reading and never let her see him with "that book" again. He had no intention of obeying that particular order.

Both boys loved books and Allen promised to share his with Eddie if Eddie would do the same and not tell. As he had with little Marse Tom, Allen gleaned whatever schooling Eddie could bring home. Textbooks were not abundant in those days. McGuffy's *Reader* taught children the simple rudiments. It is quite likely, too, that Eddie's sharing included the book that was a popular school text at the time, Lindley Murray's *English Reader*, (first published in 1828). One statement that might have penetrated his consciousness with a lifetime impression says, "The acquisition of knowledge is one of the most honorable occupations of youth."[5]

In later life Allen was to say of that period:

"Upon the discovery of my having ambition to read and write, Marse Pat and Miss Hebe. . .commenced a series of persecutions to throttle every ambition, stifle every desire and choke every aspiration that was within me to carry out the instructions of my mother to prepare myself to be a good and useful man. Many things were charged against me of which I was innocent.

"On one occasion, when the rats carried off the fresh cucumbers that had been placed on ice in the old underground icehouse, Eddie and I were charged with stealing these cucumbers. We pleaded our innocence. Miss Hebe, in order to be certain—so that the whipping she gave would be the more severe—decided to prove to us and to herself that we had eaten the cucumbers, therefore she gave each of us an emetic, a dose of ipecac.

"She stood each of us in a separate corner in her sitting room, in our shirt tails, so that our limbs would be bare and ready to receive what she intended to give us. She had two cow-hides, one painted blue, called the 'Bluebird' and one painted red, called the 'Redbird.' She used the 'Bluebird' on Eddie and the 'Redbird' on me. She sat with those two instruments of torture on her sewing table, waiting for us to surrender, as she thought we would do, the cucumbers we had eaten.

"As she was a very religious Presbyterian, she sat there humming hymns, waiting patiently for the operation of the emetic. After awhile the contents of Eddie's stomach were surrendered.

She inspected the contents of his stomach as emptied into a pail, and found no cucumbers there. This sight assisted the emetic she gave me to do its work, and soon I surrendered what I had in my stomach, and there were no cucumbers. To reward us for the pangs of this ordeal, she gave each of us a cold biscuit." [6]

Each time false accusations came at him, Allen could prove his innocence. When waiting on tables at the Pat Smith farm, the young slave saved anything left on plates uneaten. He would stash them away for later use.

"Miss Hebe," Allen in his adulthood would relate, "hunted for them when she saw the scraps were gone, took them away from me and gave them to Eddie. This favoritism to Eddie did not change our friendly relation. We had a common misery between us sufficiently strong to continue our friendship."[7] Even in the face of his own deprivation, Allen realized that brotherly love doesn't allow or include a sense of envy.

•   •   •

As the long days rolled into each other and disappeared, like bubbles in the wake of a river-boat, Allen found there were sometimes a few little moments of rare pleasure. He looked forward to the fishing season. After he had finished all his chores he sometimes got permission to take his pole and see what he could catch. Most of the "bites" he got were from mosquitoes, but he did delight in the occasional catfish he caught and cooked over hickory coals. Even then, his real satisfaction rested in being able to study his little book in privacy on the river banks.

CHAPTER 5

Almost a year had rolled by when Marse Pat Smith went back to Louisville for a visit with members of his family. During his absence, Smith left his farm, under the care of an overseer. Unknown to Smith the man was mean and cruel. He ruled the slaves under him as treacherously as a Simon Legree. All the slaves feared his unpredictable brutality. His very glance carried such a threat that the slaves lived in constant terror of even being looked at by him.

He particularly disliked Eddie and Allen. He would thrash them for the slightest infraction. One day Allen saw the overseer flogging Eddie savagely for a small and innocent deed. Every blow of the agony being inflicted on Eddie shot through Allen's body like an arrow, as memory repeated his own painful whippings. The mental anguish Allen felt at seeing a large adult man beating his young friend etched itself in his mind like impressions cut in crystal.

Sizing up the immediate situation, he determined that he would stay alert and not be caught standing around watching, or he might get the same treatment. It was just before breakfast and he had already washed himself and set the table. Casting about quickly for something to do, the first thing he thought of was to get a pan and again wash his face and hands. Immediately, he knew it was a mistake.

"BOY! What you mean by washin' yo hands after you set the table?" the angry overseer shouted.

For what seemed to be no plausible reason and with the rage of an angry bloodhound, he beat the young boy unmercifully. Added to Allen's pain was the struggle to hold back his tears.

Later, they flooded silently down his face as he put on his clothes to take the corn into town. The slightest touch was excruciating. Ugly lacerations covered his entire body.

Allen rebelled. When he got into town he decided he would never take such a flogging again.

He would run away!

The year was 1855. Allen couldn't know then, that in about six years an actual war would start which would help free the slaves. He was thirteen and determined to be free from the tyranny of men who thought they had the right to beat him so inhumanly.

On the way back to the farm he plotted his scheme. He had heard that in Canada black men were free. It was a Mecca for runaway slaves. He would go to Canada! As one former slave put it, "Canada was popular then because all of the slaves thought it was the last gate before you got all the way inside of heaven." After dinner that night, he rolled up his small blanket, added his book, his axe and all the left-over food he could gather from the kitchen.

Anxiously he waited for betraying daylight to end and bring the safety of darkness. At close to ten o'clock he decided the farm area was quiet enough for him to start his strange journey into the deep swampy woods. Beginning with a steady trot, Allen was alert and watchful as an owl soaring searchingly over the bogs.

About five miles in, the beech forest became more dense with underbrush, and he wasn't making much headway. He became drowsy and tired. He raked some dried leaves together for a bed and went to sleep.

A benevolent sun, rolling over the tree tops awakened him with its warmth early the next morning. He ate some of the food he had brought along, then packed everything else into the bundle axe and all. He left them, temporarily, at the foot of an obscure tree.

All but his little book. He didn't want to be parted from it, not even for a short while.

He headed for a farmhouse located nearby, planning to come back to find his bundle, but was never able to locate it again. At the farmhouse Allen told one of the few lies he told in his life. He said his owners, the Smiths, had gone to Louisville (true), and that they had given him permission to stay with these the new people, (not true) known to the Smiths as fellow towns-people.

His two weeks with the new family disappeared in the shadow of Allen's haunting dread of being found. Soon his welcome with them wore out.

"It's time for you to go on home now", the man of the house told him.

His fears grew more intense and tormenting. Instead of going home, he followed the snaky, picturesque bends of the Ohio River. He made his way back into the town of Henderson, where he thought he could get lost in the crowd of other slaves. Roaming the streets of the bustling town, he momentarily enjoyed the luxury of doing just what he pleased. Suddenly a notorious slave hunter spotted him as a runaway slave.

The trader grabbed him, strapped him to a mule, tied his hands behind him and secured his body with rings under mule's belly. In this discomfort they returned to the Pat Smith plantation. Fortunately for Allen, the cruel overseer was out in the fields when they arrived.

After being locked in an old smokehouse, he worried over his next move. Somehow his friend Eddie found him there.

"That old overseer's looking for you good", Eddie told his friend. "He's telling everybody 'if that scoundrel is ever caught and brought back to the farm I intend to tie him to a barrel, strip him naked and lash him with a cat-o-nine-tails soaked in salt water'."

Such a horrible fate Allen could easily imagine, actually almost feel. His only resource was in remembering his mother's advice, "When in trouble son, look to the Lord." So he did just that, because he knew he was in **big** trouble. He prayed to God to help him find a way out.

Soon, as if in direct answer to his prayers, he spotted over in the corner, an old shovel, half buried in the dirt floor. He quickly used the shovel to pry open the lock on the smokehouse door and burst out. FREE.

Well, not exactly free, for there, sitting on the veranda not far from the smoke-house sat aunt Phyllis, the housekeeper, and aunt Betty, the cook. Allen managed to sneak unseen around the back of the servants' cabin. From there he could hear the goings on in the big house. He was sure aunt Phyllis and the cook wouldn't betray him.

The slave hunter and overseer went to the smokehouse, only to find the lock broken and their prey gone. Exuding the venom of an angry water moccasin, the overseer inquired of the two women on the veranda. They both vowed at this time they had neither seen nor heard anything.

The vengeful overseer went into town, returned with a pack of bloodhounds and put them on Allen's trail. The young slave went racing through the forest like a chased 'possum. At times the slave-hunters got so close Allen heard the dogs barking and baying behind him. Though he had not had a bath for a month, the hounds couldn't pick up his scent! Allen knew it was the Lord's protecting power watching over him.

Had he heard of the intricate Underground Railroad that operated in secret through many of the Southern states, Allen's escape would have been insured. Thousands of slaves received housing, food, transportation and kindness through this highly successful volunteer operation. But totally alone, he made his own perilous way through the entanglements.

Escaping the dogs, Allen hid in that area for another two weeks. But captivity overtook him again. This time by way of Aunt Betty, the cook. She had figured out where he might be hiding and told the overseer. Why she had betrayed her young friend, Allen would never know.

He did know she had reported him though, and before anyone could catch up with him he quickly escaped and ran away again. This time he stopped at another nearby plantation. Hunger gnawed at his insides so hard he felt weak. It was Saturday and he had eaten nothing for two days. He hid in the hay loft of this house until darkness came, then headed back to the town of Henderson, and the house of other slaves he knew.

He begged them for something to eat and they gave him a bit of hoe cake and a large slice of fat meat. They insisted he leave fast before the white folks saw him. To him the crude meal was a feast as satisfying as the coon pie and crackling bread his mother used to make.

Despite his full stomach luck was evading him once again. He brashly walked the streets of Henderson the next day. The family physician of the Smiths, his real owners recognized him. Dr. Jones housed him safely until Pat Smith and his wife, Hebe, returned from Louisville. On his return, Smith heard of his young slave's rebellion and decided he didn't want him back. He gave Dr. Jones orders to have him sold to the first slave hunter who wanted him.

Allen had become a strong, handsome, capable lad, mature for his age. Displayed on the steps of the courthouse, he sold quickly, like a piece of horse-flesh, to a Martin Hancock. For 960 dollars! Glad to live in the city for a change, Allen thought he had a permanent home here with the Hancocks in Henderson.

One morning, however, Martin Hancock took him, without explanation to the teeming steamboat landing nearby. Allen realized that, once again, he was going down the river. Hancock owned numbers of slaves, and shunting them around like cattle, he took them to the slave market in Memphis, Tennessee. It was a long journey, down the Ohio River to where it joins the Mississippi and on down to the southwestern part of Tennessee.

Bearing the new price of twelve hundred dollars, Allen stood around in chains in the steamy Memphis market for a week without anyone offering money for him. One day a slave driver came by and herded him, with a number of other slaves, back to the boat landing and shipped them off down the Mississippi to New Orleans, Louisiana. Crowded against chained bodies, in heat that seemed it could fry corn pone, Allen didn't realize that this was much the same manner in which his ancestors arrived from Africa around 1619.

In those days, white sea captains rounded up boatloads of already captured Africans and brought them to Jamestown, Virginia to sell to wealthy plantation owners. Many of the poor souls thought they were being brought to this country to be eaten. They were quickly sold, and the diabolical situation arose in which one human being thinks he can own another, as a man owns a dog or a horse. Slave trading had begun in the United States.

At the slave mart in New Orleans, in the mid 1800's, Allen competed with over a thousand other slaves waiting for a master. They were classified according to their ability and put in the deplorable "nigger pen", seated on benches like rows of canned goods on a market shelf. There they sat until the gas lights went on. All were eager to be sold so they wouldn't have to endure the tortures and indignities forced on them by the traders, who were even more treacherous than the worst slave holders.

A round, bald and chubby man named Scruggs walked up to the trader and said he was looking for a jockey. His eye fell on the slightly built Allen. He made the young man jump and move to make sure he was agile enough for the job. Finally, after bargaining and bickering, Scruggs bought the slave at the reduced price of a thousand dollars. Scruggs, a horse racer, used slaves to operate his many large stables. His reputation said that he treated his slaves well. He fed them adequately, and was gentle with them. They never knew when he would sell them for a higher price than he paid. He gambled on everything, including his servants. He gave Allen a new suit of clothes and the young man had a hint of the same pleasureable feeling of worth he had with Mrs. Talbot, the Quaker lady in Louisville.

Running away!

CHAPTER 6

Allen felt an even greater feeling of self-esteem when
"Marse" Fred Scruggs put him in charge of exercising his prized
horse, "Red Oak". Scruggs allowed him to hold the reins while they
drove around town, carrying on business in the stores. This added
responsibility nourished his growing sense of selfhood. He gained
skill as a jockey here with Scruggs. Out of all his extraordinary
life accomplishments, one encyclopedia lists him merely as a
"famed jockey".

Allen made great strides in his ability to read. Because of his
later dedication to religion, it's safe to assume he read the Bible
whenever he got the chance. By the time Scruggs bought him, he
could easily recognize street names and numbers. One warm
afternoon Scruggs discovered this talent in the boy, much to his
surprise. Did he explode in anger as Allen's other owners had done?

No, being a much kinder, more intelligent man, it gave him a
feeling of pride. He realized he had one of the smarter "boys" to
be had on the slave market. When it came to his thought to sell
Allen he took him to a slave trader from Jackson, Mississippi. In
order to get a higher price for him, Scruggs extolled Allen's ability
to read street signs, etc. in order to get a better price. He had Allen
read to the man.

Instead of being impressed the man turned down the sale.

"I don't want no boy that can read. I like him but he's too smart."

So Scruggs sold the man a younger and not so ambitious lad.
Deciding to keep Allen on a little longer, Scruggs told him they were
to move to Louisville where a famous race track could show off his

horses. (It is believed by some that this was a forerunner to the Kentucky Derby, established in Louisville in 1875.)

Rumbles of war drums were echoing now in the South. The Union Army who, among other things, wanted to free the slaves, formed blockades on the Mississippi river in Memphis,Tennessee. Southern Confederates, who didn't want to give up their slaves were rousing to fight for their holdings.

Long before Allen became aware of the conflict on behalf of the slaves, and even before he was born, many conscientious white writers and thinkers had been voicing their objections to slavery. John Greenleaf Whittier, Henry Ward Beecher, and Charles Sumner were just a few. They were writers who, through the years, had helped to shape the thoughts of people toward rights and freedom for all men equally. A movement had begun as early as 1786, when George Washington said ". . . among my first wishes [is] to see some plan adopted by which slavery in this country may be abolished by law"[5]. This movement spread in ever growing numbers of people who wanted to bring about the abolition of slavery. Among slave owners were those who rejected it as an impractical and foolish disturbing of the peace.

Northern and Southern states began gathering their forces for the events which history was to call the Civil War. In a Chicago speech on July 10, 1858, Abraham Lincoln said, "Let us discard all this quibbling about this man and the other man, this race and that race and the other race being inferior, and therefore they must be placed in an inferior position. Let us discard all these things and unite as one person throughout this land, until we shall once more stand up declaring that all men are created equal." (ibid)

One man, familiar to United States history felt drawn to these words enough to fight to the death for them was John Brown, a

Kansan and militant abolitionist. He took sixteen white men (including his two sons and himself) and five blacks on a raid at Harper's Ferry, Virginia. The history of his bloody battle which ended with his being hanged for treason has been immortalized in poems and songs. It is believed to have helped bring on the Civil War.

The dark clouds of battle had not yet burst officially into their ghastly terror when the steamer carrying Allen, Scruggs and his band of trainers, jockeys, horses and slaves landed in Louisville. The animals and baggage found a home in a livery stable. The slaves had their choice of where, in the hay loft above, they wanted to light. It would be a few feet they could call their bedrooms. Scruggs saw to it that they were fed at a nearby hotel.

Allen was elated to be once again in Louisville, which had now become the tenth largest city in the United States. The coming of May had edged the bluegrass on the rolling hills with smoky blue flowers. The air fragrantly acknowledged that day's early rain. But the thoughts of seeing his dear mother for the first time in several years, lifted his spirits the most.

His search for the one person in the world he loved, began with an anxious trip to his birthplace, the plantation of his earliest owners, the Starbirds. The windowless shack where he was born still stood. A straggling weed grew inside on the dirt floor, nourished by rain from the leaky roof. It seemed a lifetime of Springs since he had left the old place.

A wave of glad emotion welled up in his heart on hearing from the Starbirds that his mother had obtained her freedom. It became a bittersweet feeling and a down pulling surge of sadness swept over him when he learned that her freedom came because she was of no more use to her owners. Her sight was dimming, they told him, and the shadow of creeping feebleness hung over her. She had left the Starbirds and her whereabouts were not known to them.

In her heart, Phyllis still cherished hopes of finding some of her lost children. She had gone to New Orleans to look for them. Allen learned that she would soon be returning to Louisville. In the meantime he turned his efforts toward finding his sister, Mary Jane, Phyllis' oldest daughter who had remained somewhere in Louisville.

Again grief and despondency engulfed Allen when he found Mary Jane, freed from slavery but totally blind and penniless. She lived in a shabby, though rent free lean-to. He felt even more melancholy on hearing her experiences. Years later he related the sad story to a friend:

"Her master agreed to let her have her freedom on the payment to him, in a designated period of time, of twelve hundred dollars. To earn this amount of money in the time allotted, {she} realized that she must work night and day. . . She performed all sorts of labor; she took in washing and ironing during the day, and sewing at night. Her struggles were unceasing. She would sew by a dim light nearly all night, take a little rest, and then, rising early in the morning, would start about her washing and ironing.

"This unusual strain and taxation upon her energies and her eyes soon told on her health. Her eyesight was rapidly failing. . . until finally the light faded away entirely, and she was left in utter darkness. The master, knowing full well that she was helpless, that her days of usefulness had gone by, proposed that he would release her on the payment of all the money she had accumulated, which amounted to eight hundred dollars. She gladly surrendered to him all her money." She was free, but helpless without income.

The gloom in Allen's heart on hearing his sister's story lasted several days. Soon his mother arrived back in Louisville, having caught the last train the Confederates allowed through their fast forming lines. Her daughter told her of Allen's presence in town, and she made haste toward the livery stable where he lived. He, at the same time hastened on his way to Mary Jane's for the meeting with his mother.

In a dramatic, tearfully joyful coincidence they happened to meet on the street about half way between their destinations. Allen was smitten speechless.

"Oh thankie Jesus, Thankie Jesus." His mother uttered the words through her usual tears of gratitude. She repeated them over and over as she clung to the son she thought she would never see again. "Thankie Jesus! You sho' has heard my humble prayer; you sho' has heard my prayer. You kept my boy and done brought him back to me. Oh thankie." Her hands, gnarled and knotted from her labors, trembled as she squeezed her son's arm in poignant affection.

Catching up on the lost years, his mother told him how she had found another of her children. Living in New Orleans she often visited the parish prison to cheer the inmates and talk religion to them. In those days in many parts of the South , besides being a crime to teach Negroes to read and write, it was also illegal to give them any religious instruction. This was objected to for the following reasons, according to one source:

"1. If we suffer our Negroes to be instructed, the tendency will be to change the civil relations of society as now constituted.

2. The way will be opened for men from abroad to enter in and inculcate doctrines subversive to our interests and safety.

3. The religious instruction of the Negroes will lead to neglect of duty and insubordination.

4. The Negroes will embrace seasons of religious worship

for originating and executing plans of insubordination and villainy.

5. Religious instruction will do no good; it will only make the Negroes worse men and worse hypocrites."

If Allen's mother knew of these objections she chose to ignore them in order to give "the Lord's word" to the helpless prisoners. She soon learned the names of all the prisoners.

One day as she distributed snacks to the unfortunates she saw a face she hadn't seen there before. It was her son Major! She tried to maintain her composure, and mastering her grievous longing to reach through the bars and embrace him, she casually asked him why he was there.

The twenty years since they had seen each other had brought horrible tortures to her son. Without seeming to recognize her he told her he was due to receive fifty bare back lashes for reading a newspaper to his master's house-girl. When his master found that his slave could read he became enraged, and had Major committed to the prison. He was to receive the fifty lashes for simply being able to read! And she could do nothing for him.

Soon, after Allen and his mother had exchanged tales of their woes and triumphs over the last years, he had to go back to his livery stable in town and she to her daughter's house. They were able to get together on many occasions while he lived in the vicinity of Louisville, and she became again, a bright spot in Allen's life.

A biographer who knew Allen in later life said in 1914, "Even to this day Allensworth speaks of his mother with a tenderness, an affection that shows that God endowed him with that beautiful, mysterious love characteristic of the most cultivated white man."[8]

Chapter 7

In the spring of 1861 the War Between the States began in earnest. Abraham Lincoln was the sixteenth president of the Union. Just five days after Allen's nineteenth birthday the Confederates fired cannons on the soldiers of Fort Sumter, a U.S. Army (Union) fortification in the harbor of Charleston, South Carolina.

For 34 hours, history tells us, guns bombarded Fort Sumter. No one was killed, but the Civil War started in earnest. There followed four years of bloody battles, with men killing their brother-man over political considerations as well as the slavery question. They were battles that changed history, maps and men. Historical accounts of the era are laden with many fierce contests like those at Gettysburg, Fort Sumter and Bull Run, each with its own heroes.

There were no heroes in Allen's life when the war started. It did change major directions of his life, though. Marse Scruggs had great plans for the horses under Allen's care. In the Fall they were to race at a popular track near Louisville. News of the coming battle canceled all races, and Scruggs left for the North on a business trip. He placed his horses and slaves for safe keeping until he needed them again. They were put in the hands of Jim Ficklin, a fierce overseer on a farm about 15 miles from Louisville.

On Ficklin's farm Allen found a number of kindred souls, also from Louisville. Like Allen, these were unusual young men who had been punished severely by their masters for attempting to get knowledge and learning. They banded together to encourage each other in their search for education.

Some among these friends, however, ignorantly believed in

superstition as a way to get rid of some of their problems. Their hatred for Ficklin's merciless treatment of them led a few of the slaves to try do away with him by black magic. They somehow got from Ficklin's house a daguerreotype picture of the overseer. They covered it with ink and buried it in the ground where they thought people would trample over it and Ficklin would dwindle to death. Ficklin didn't die, of course.

Not long after this, the group enticed Allen into joining in another scheme to destroy the cruel overseer through voodooism. They believed that if they could get a lock of the person's hair, make a hole in a hickory tree and put the hair in it, the owner would die of a headache. In his adulthood, Allensworth, in slightly embarrassed remembrance of the notions of superstition he was temporarily fooled by, told the story:

"I watched Marse Jim getting a hair cut. . .and got my wished for lock of hair. With an auger I went to the woods where I found a big hickory tree; I bored the hole; [and put in the hair] . . . took great pains to make an oak peg to fit it perfectly; drove it in tight; cut it off smooth, and rubbed some mud over the place, and patiently waited to hear Marse Jim say, 'I have a headache'. But his head never ached. . . and he never died either." Allen must have lost all faith in such "cures" from then on.

Though overseer Jim Ficklin showed himself to be a heartless person, life on his farm did give Allen opportunities and experiences he had never had before. His regular duties depended on the weather. In good weather they were the usual farm and livery stable duties. In rainy weather, after he had done his usual exercising of the horses, shucking of corn, and hulling the peas, he learned to repair shoes with new soles and heels. This was the first skill other than farm and stable duties Allen ever learned. He discovered he had mechanical ability. He had learned something new!

Another opportunity appeared when some of the slaves invited him to join their "orchestra." Allen learned to play all the musical instruments the group could scrounge. He mastered the triangle, the crude snare drums, Jews harp, bones and tambourine. None of his friends could afford a banjo so popular in those days. With its plunka-plunka-plunk it normally added to the melody. Their voices provided the tunes. They didn't therefore, make much actual music with these tuneless instruments but Allensworth did learn the proper beat and cadence.

This understanding helped him when the slaves organized secret country dances; secret because some churches and their members felt that dancing and religion did not belong together. Thus dancing was forbidden in some parts of the South. In order to ease the conscience of dancers at Christmas festivities one member would be appointed to "beg a blessing on the dance".

In a poem written around 1858 regarding this blessing are the words:*

> "We have no ark to dance afore,
> like Israel's prophet king
> But according to the rights we have
> we do the best we knows
> And folks don't despise the violet-flower
> because it ain't no rose."

The few hours of pleasure gained from their "cake walkin" lured Allen into a crafty and dishonest practice, not natural to his normal tendencies.

The slaves lived in such deadly fear of their masters that they would never dare to exhibit any kind of fun as joyful as dancing anywhere near the plantation. But they could sometimes get permission to go 'possum hunting. So they would plan ahead, buy a couple of 'possums in town because it would be almost impossible to come back empty handed from a 'possum hunt. Then they would go out on their free time and dance their hearts out. Allen had the important position of "caller". Back on the farm they would share one 'possum with their owners and no one was the wiser.

At other times when they took the corn to be ground at the mill, they would gather at some spot along the road and jig for an hour or two. The two methods were innocent but downright deceptions and Allen knew it, but he could be forgiven for a few moments of merriment in such a dark life. Even though dark, things were getting brighter every day for the young man.

It so happened that Marse Jim Ficklin did his banking in the town of Louisville, at the Bank of Kentucky. One day the bank president, Virgil McKnight asked Ficklin if he had, among his boys, one who might be good as a house servant. Ficklin immediately thought of Allen. He remembered being told of Allen's previous service as waiter and server. It isn't clear whether Ficklin sold Allen, or simply let him go. In light of later events, it's probable that he merely let him go and got in trouble with Pat Smith, Allen's still legal owner.

Allen's heart sang with joy when he found he was going to the McKnight's. Their home was nearer to Louisville and he hoped he might get to see his dear mother. Besides that, he would get to wear nicer clothes than his grubby stable garb. The clothes furnished him were all altered hand-me-downs from the rotund Virgil McKnight. There was enough fabric in the over-sized man's pants alone to make a handsome suit for Allen. He was so neatly clad that some of the other slaves soon considered Allen a dandy.

During his stay at the McKnights' farm, Allen's indoor chores kept him busy and fairly happy. He would often find himself humming one of the familiar church hymns his mother taught him, like *Rock of Ages, Truth divine,* which first appeared in *The Gospel Magazine* in 1776. He paid little attention to the military activity amassing around Louisville.

* From American Negro Slavery by Irwin Russell

CHAPTER 8

Aware or not, the war was closing in on young Allensworth. It was 1862 and Confederate General Braxton Bragg was marching toward Louisville in an effort to take over the Union State of Kentucky. Allen lived just within the Federal jurisdiction. Military people camped all around the countryside in tents and make-shift shelters. One day Allen met a Union officer with whom he became friends. He related to the officer his life as a slave, his sorrows, pains, his hopes and his unsuccessful attempts to run away.

The officer arranged for Allen to become temporarily attached to the Forty-fourth Infantry (Illinois) Hospital Corps, as a civilian nurse, taking care of the wounded in his area. This first step in another attempt at freedom came about because of his desire to serve his fellow man. However, way down in the back of his thought there lurked the hope, that this might lead him to his desired status, and perhaps, even to Canada!

When the group was ordered to the front, Allen marched with them to Louisville, along the Salt River Road and up Main Street, a path that would take them past Virgil McKnight's bank. To keep from being recognized, Allen took off his good clothes and disguised himself in an old soldier's suit. He put a kettle on his head for a helmet, and spread mud all over his face. With his head held straight ahead while his eyes focused on the bank he marched right past McKnight who stood on the bank's porch.

Being a nurse with the army, though not as bad as slavery, brought its equivalent in emotional pain to Allen. He was under as direct orders from the Doctor as from slave owners. On the move constantly, the Corps set up meager hospital tents and shacks with straw floors. In some of the hospitals, food was so scarce that they lived on hardtack, beans and bacon. Allensworth made up his mind to do his best in everything. It was one of the characteristics that ultimately made him great. His deep, innate compassion brought a sense of satisfaction in giving comfort to the wounded.

Witnessing and dressing their wounds was bearable until the Corps got to the back end of General Bragg's army. The picture changed for the worse. Both blue and gray clad soldiers in mutilated, and in hideous forms of near-death caused anguish to the sympathetic nurse. Their screams of pain, and cries for help caused Allensworth to feel their suffering vicariously as he had when he saw his friend Eddie's thrashing years earlier.

In December of that year, General Bragg lost his battle, and retreated. Fighting ceased in that particular spot. The Hospital Company headed South toward Nashville, Tennessee and took Allen with them. At a camp on the way, Allen met some friends, one of whom informed him that his old overseer, Jim Ficklin, was looking for him. Ficklin must have realized the quality of help Allen was capable of and wanted him back. Or perhaps he was embarrassed to have let the slave, who actually still belonged to Fred Scruggs, get away.

Whatever the cause, dread again struck the slave-heart of Allen who had thought he was free from that element. By using wily and crafty means Ficklin tried his best to get at Allen by infiltrating the encampment. The doctor in charge, to whom Allen confided his fears, convinced him that he could not legally be taken from his work there unless he really wanted to go.

Allen easily made it clear that he did *not* want to go. The Colonel who commanded the hospital camp heard of the scheming and had Ficklin hooted and jeered out of the camp by the troops. So overjoyed was Allen at this his first real triumph over the hated system of slavery that he said aloud, "Thank the Lord."

Throughout winter's cold, snows and distress, the Union and the Confederate armies were often only about a mile away from Allen's temporary hospital quarters. He could hear guns from both sides. Often he would see the orange fire spitting out from the rifles. Ever present smoky clouds wafted whichever way the wind sent them. By December 31 the Hospital Corps, driven from their position, decided again to retreat to protect their wounded.

Allen caught one of the unmounted horses running away from the Cavalry, and being the expert rider that he had become as a jockey for Fred Scruggs, rode the remaining fearsome miles to Nashville, praying all the way. There he reported to a general hospital under Dr. A.J. Gordon, where he knew he could be of service.

Stretchers brought the wounded in hourly, in ghastly, heart-breaking numbers. Doctors and nurses worked day and night. Moments of dark depression would sometimes settle over Allen as somber as a moonless night on the prairie. Would he or his countrymen ever find peace of mind? Soon the injured soldiers became more in number than could be accommodated by the facilities available. The Officer in Charge put them on board an Army Commissary steamer, the *St. Patrick* and sent them North, with Dr. Gordon, to Evansville, Indiana. Again Allen went along as a nurse.

When the boat docked at Evansville, Allen suddenly felt free to walk around the city. It was the first real freedom he had ever known. His senses soared higher than the bald eagles he'd seen in the trees from the steamer deck. He imagined this was what Canada would feel like. Although his urgent *need* to get there waned, his desire was still strong. Allen's love of learning would naturally guide him to seek out the library in any city he entered. He kept up with his reading, always broadening the scope of his interests. His very pores sponged up knowledge. Slave owners would often say that slaves were not capable of being educated, but Allen was proving them wrong.

He quickly became good friends with Dr. Gordon who recognized the young man's worthiness and fine character. Allen accepted the doctor's invitation to visit his family in Georgetown, Ohio. Even though he was only about a hundred miles northeast of Louisville he had never felt closer to Canada than now. He didn't admit even to himself that the dream had lost some of its urgency.

The city of Georgetown filled Allen with awe and excitement. Ohio was considered a border state and escaped the brunt of the war battles. Here he was, in a private home, a neat, well-furnished room, welcomed by the family, eating at their table and treated as a free person! We can imagine his exultation. He had sometimes felt he would never be free. Often the dejection and discouragement had overwhelmed him. The melancholy and hopelessness had seemed to come as tides that swept over him. Often, though the tides ebbed out due to some of the little kindnesses he experienced. Now he was free in the land of the free! He felt like a gentleman, his own man at last.

•   •   •

In April 1863 the War Between the States reached unthinkable heights. On January 1 of that year Abraham Lincoln rocked the nation with his Emancipation Proclamation. This document, so important to the shape of Black history, today lies in the National Archives, faded and yellowed, and unseen by the largest proportion of Americans. Far from the lofty words and inspiration of the Gettysburg Address, for example, its message is bogged down in law-document language. However, the intent is unmistakable,

"*. . . by virtue of the power and for the purpose aforesaid"*, it reads in part, *"I do order and declare that all persons held as slaves within said designated States and parts of States, are, and henceforward shall be free; and that the Executive Government of the United States, including the military and naval authorities thereof, will recognize and maintain the freedom of said persons.*

"And I hereby enjoin upon the people so declared to be free to abstain from all violence, unless in necessary self-defense; and I recommend to them that, in all cases when allowed, they labor faithfully for reasonable wages.

And I further declare and make known that such persons of suitable condition will be received into the armed service of the United States, to garrison forts, positions, stations, and other places and to man vessels of all sorts in said service. (Emphasis, added.)

Allen rejoiced over this declaration of freedom for his people. He was twenty-one, already free, and thinking seriously about his life. The war raged on. Allen realized it might be years before equality joined the hands of blacks and whites. At the same time he wanted to pay back the government for some of the good experiences he had as a civilian with the Army. It may have been the words in the Emancipation Proclamation about military and naval activities and manning "vessels of all sorts" that led him to his next decision.

On April 3, 1863 he signed up as a First Class Seaman for a two year stint in the Navy. He was stationed on the *Queen City*, one of the gun-boats fitted up for service on the Mississippi. He now received a regular salary. Eighteen dollars a month!

On the *Queen City*, Allensworth had two black friends, whose attitude was much different from his. These were young Afro-Americans born into slavery, who had never known any kind of reason for doing right except to stave off punishment. Few were ever rewarded for a job well done; their sense of right and wrong as yet undeveloped. They became discontented with the confining life on board ship, anchored in mid-river so they couldn't go ashore. They planned to jump ship. As soon as they got the chance, they deserted, leaving Allen the only Black man on the ship.

As they silently slid over the ship's rail Allen's emotions tore at him. Should he join them? It wasn't too late. Temptations screamed in his ears like banshees. He wanted a good time as much as they did. But he was a man of honor, as was to be proven in all his military life. He stayed.

Aboard the *Queen City* steaming up and down in the dangerous waters, Allen won the respect of the Captain as well as his fellow seamen. Soon he was promoted to Captain's steward with a First Class Petty Officer rating and a salary of thirty-five dollars a month! His experience as cabin boy on the steamer *Rainbow* years ago paid off. He even got to use the dinghy to go ashore when duties permitted. On one of the shore trips he bought his mother two good warm blankets. He always sent her part of his monthly salary.

Later transferred to another boat, the *Tawah*, he was part of a fleet patrolling the Tennessee river from Paducah to the Muscle Shoals in Alabama. Dodging heavy gunfire raining down from the river banks, they crossed and re-crossed the river destroying Confederate boats. As the shells whizzed past him day and night Allen had moments of panic. He narrowly escaped death more than once. But always, afterwards, he would say to himself, "Mother must surely be praying for me tonight, she must surely be praying for me!" He himself prayed often for his life and reverently offered prayers of thanks for being delivered from the destruction that was so harrowingly near.

Throughout all his tours of duty, the young man fostered and indulged his strong desire to know more, to read more, and to learn more. It guided and prodded him his whole lifetime. The *Tawah* was destroyed at Johnsonville, Tennessee, leaving few records behind. It is known that Allensworth later joined the crew on the *Cincinnati,* his last service before his tour of duty was up.

The Cincinnati gun boat on which Allensworth served during the
Civil War.

CHAPTER 9

On April 4, 1865 Allen completed his short term of enlistment
and was discharged from the Navy. Just five days later, General Lee
surrendered and ended the horrid battles of the Civil War. It was the
battle which killed so many to *free* so many, and helped win a new
life for slaves. Ten days after Allensworth left the Navy, Abraham
Lincoln was assassinated. Just a month earlier, in his Second
Inaugural Address the President had said, "With malice toward none;
with charity for all; with firmness in the right, as God gives us to
see the right, let us strive on to finish the work we are in. . ."

There were eons of work to do before equal rights for all men
would be realized, but the slaves were free men, by government
decree at least. Fortunately, the Navy had brought early release for
Allensworth. He had served his post with proficiency and a sense
of honor.

His heart pounded as fast as a trip-hammer and a flush of
well-being swept over him when he was handed his discharge papers.
He found they included a large amount of discharge pay from the
Navy and a lump sum from the government.

He immediately thought of his mother.

Back in Louisville, again in May, the blue grass he loved was
at its bluest, and the familiar cardinals flashed and flitted overhead
as he had remembered them. Allen headed straight to the ramshackle
little hovel where his mother lived. She had regained her health,
and stood steadier on her feet than the last time they were together.
And he shouldn't have been surprised to see her burst into her

usual tears at the first dim sight of him. They both knew that these were tears of jubilant gladness. She had lived to see her favorite son a free man! The two knelt in prayer and thanksgiving to God for his wonderful kindness, before Allen had to leave once again.

•   •   •

For the next two years Allen worked as a civilian employee of the Navy, wherever they needed him. By then he had saved enough money to go into business for himself. He found one of his long lost brothers, William, in St. Louis, Missouri. Together they opened a restaurant on Market Street. Allen's background of preparing and serving food on board the steamer and in owners' homes gave him a good foundation for this new venture.

At the outset, however, unscrupulous operators threatened the enterprise. Seeking to rent a piece of property as a storeroom Allen paid an exorbitant sum for the first month's rent. Two days later he was told that the owner wouldn't rent to him because of his color. Then the brothers were accused of passing counterfeit money. When the police were brought in by the perpetrators they sized up the situation and on good evidence, refused to take Allen or his brother to jail. If they had gone to prison the consequences could have ruined Allensworth's life prospects and prevented him from accomplishing his outstanding usefulness to his fellow man.

The new restaurateurs prospered despite such set-backs. They became famous for their gumbo, potted veal and gooseberry pie. Soon the business was so successful they moved to larger quarters, and within a year, opened up a second restaurant.

Allen discovered within himself a business sense that had contributed to their success and acclaim. One day a man came by with an exceptionally inviting offer to buy the business. The brothers sold, and Allen returned to his hometown of Louisville. It surprised him to see how the town had grown. The streets were broad, lovely homes with beautiful gardens abounded; carriages with liveried Negro footmen fancied up the streets and everything had a more prosperous look.

•   •   •

For a man who loved his Bible, and being as addicted to learning as Allensworth, it was understandable that his desire for employment might turn somehow to religion. He had always loved hearing his mother telling him what few stories she knew of Bible characters, such as Moses, Jesus and probably Daniel in the lion's den. Then one evening, he sat silently alone in his room, with his Bible in his lap, contemplating his life's direction. Gradually, there settled over him what seemed to be a gentle but all encompassing beam of brilliant light. Its radiance flooded his consciousness with the unshakable realization that his love for God was the most important thing in his life. A peace more comforting than he had ever known before engulfed him. He felt as close to God as breathing.

A prolonged, unselfed feeling of serenity, joy and gratitude surrounded him him. The experience brought an unquestionable sense of direction. In his words, "he got religion". He promptly joined Louisville's Fifth Street Baptist Church.

Allen began a diligent search for employment in order to buy his food and clothing and support his mother. The American Missionary Society of New York had started building schools around the South. Allen heard that they were building one right there in Louisville. He quickly applied for a job as janitor and was accepted. At the same time he registered as a pupil. He was 25 years old.

His experience at the Ely Normal School winged his thoughts in anticipation of his future prospects. Reputable schools of his day included character building, ethics and elocution. It would be safe to conclude that his earliest textbooks included the now famous Lindley Murray Reader. The exact title the 1828 school book so widely used in Allen's day was, *English Reader*; or PIECES IN PROSE AND VERSE *from the* BEST WRITERS *designed* to ASSIST YOUNG PERSONS TO READ WITH PROPRIETY AND EFFECT; *Improve Their Language and Sentiments; and To Inculcate The Most Important Principles of PIETY AND VIRTUE, with a few preliminary OBSERVATIONS ON THE PRINCIPLES of GOOD READING.* (Capital letters theirs). Lindley Murray would have been proud of Allen Allensworth who took the words to heart.

Life was very busy and full for the janitor/student. He arose before six every morning, and walked eleven blocks to the school. He would clean seven rooms in the building, attend class and walk back home in the afternoon to study. Meshed in with all this were the household chores he did in the boarding house where he lived rent free in return for his labor. He never forgot to send his mother all the money he could afford.

Allen remained at the Normal School until in 1865, when the Freedmen's Bureau started providing schools for freed slaves. Under the War Department the Bureau endeavored to meet the heavy demands of those who wanted to learn to read and write. On the basis that "only a proper education stood between the Negro and an equal place in American Society", the non-sectarian association established over 4000 schools.

"It was a whole race trying to go to school", Booker T. Washington said. "Few were too young and none too old to make the attempt to learn. Not only the day schools were filled, but night schools as well. The great ambition of the older people was to try to learn to read the Bible before they died."

Major Ben Runkle, Officer in Charge of staffing the Bureau's schools requested Ely Normal School's Principle, Professor Hamilton's help in finding a teacher for a Freedmen's school. The school was in Christmasville, a few miles south of Louisville. Hamilton had admired the outstanding work of Allen so it wasn't surprising that he recommended the young man.

The recommendation surprised no one but Allen himself. He could hardly imagine himself teaching others while he was still striving for more education. He accepted the job with great trepidation. He was confident, however of his ability to keep his group of active boys in line. He was born into forced obedience, as a slave, and his Navy experience demanded strict discipline. That part of teaching didn't frighten him. He knew he could get whatever else he needed from books. Many things he learned from his Lindley Murray Reader must have helped him in his teaching. For example, "What a sculptor is to a block of marble, education is to a human soul." This was a reference to the ancient philosophy of Aristotle who felt that a beautiful statue is already in the block of marble awaiting only the artist's hands to chip away the rubble and polish the stone. In this case the marble is the human mind. They were words that would have penetrated deeply into his thoughts to be used throughout his career, which was to include much educating of young people.

By the time 1871 came around, the elders and officers of his Church, the Fifth Street Baptist Church of Louisville, sensed the evidence of deep spirituality in Allensworth. On an April Sunday, two days after his twenty-ninth birthday, the whole congregation gathered and celebrated his appointment as preacher of the Gospel to their churches. The Civil War hostility was over in the minds of most Kentuckians, and traveling about the South was no longer dangerous. Allensworth successfully journeyed throughout the state as a missionary and teacher. This included special assignments to preach in Cave City and Hopkinsville.

He was pleased and perhaps a little proud to be in this position. Still he had an ever present, reverent humility balancing his pride. In his own mind, he could not believe that he was equal to many of his students. They would often ask questions he couldn't answer. That little goad still sat on his shoulders urging him to learn more, learn more, learn MORE. At this period the focus was to find out more about God and the Christianity he was to preach.

He prayed his way into the Baptist Theological Institute in Nashville, Tennessee. (Established in 1864, this school for Negroes was early re-named the Roger Williams University and the name remained until the school was closed in 1931).

Reverend D.W. Phillips, D.D., President of the Institute, knew that Allensworth could barely afford the tuition. He accepted the young man's application anyway. In partial return for the tuition, Allensworth wrote "letters of a missionary character" for the Judson Missionary Society of the Second Baptist Church in Cleveland, Ohio.

In a letter similar to those from Allensworth, one minister reported back to the Society about his summer vacation activities. He spoke despairingly of the conduct of some of the pastors and teachers as did Rev. Allensworth. He related instances of corruption and immorality in the personal lives of those responsible for Bible teaching and preaching.

'With Allensworth-style optimism, however, he wrote, "But still there is hope amid all these discouragements. These Institutions of learning are springs of living water which send forth refreshing streams over the wild waste. They are constantly sending forth young men and women who carry the light to the people who are sitting in the shadow of death. They are accomplishing much for both young and old".*

The aspiring Bible student came out of the Institute as *Reverend* Allensworth, a fully ordained minister with a degree in Theology! The little slave boy had triumphed over the limitations of ignorance, lack of education, lack of opportunity and personal freedom, emerging out of the darkness that would try to punish him for the way he was born. But this was only the beginning.

* Portion of an undated letter from the files of Henry Lyman Morehouse, corresponding Secretary of The American Baptist Home Mission Society. Used with permission of the American Baptist Historical Society, Valley Forge, Pennsylvania.

TEACHER'S CERTIFICATE.

"AS IS THE TEACHER, SO WILL BE THE SCHOOL."

State of Kentucky, _City of Bowling Green_ County, &:

Allen Allensworth having presented satisfactory evidence of good moral character, and having passed an examination in Spelling, Reading, Writing, Arithmetic, Grammar, Geography, History of the United States, and Composition, with the results indicated in the annexed Class and Grade, is, hereby, granted a Certificate as a qualified Teacher for the Common Schools of said City County for the term of _One_ years.

GRADE _1st_ CLASS _1st_ EXPIRES _March 12th, 1886_

Spelling	65	History of the United States	90
Reading	95	Composition	79
Writing	75	Theory and Practice of Teaching	95
Written Arithmetic	55	School Laws	
Mental Arithmetic	56	Has Taught 36 Months	
Grammar	76	Takes 1 Educational Journal	
Geography	51	General Average 75.7	

EXPLANATIONS.

General Average is made on the eight Common School Branches, viz.: Spelling, Reading, Writing, Arithmetic, Grammar, Geography, History of the United States, and Composition, but may be modified by other evidences of professional ability. The scale of gradation is 100. A percentage of 90 entitles a Teacher to a First Grade, First Class Certificate; a percentage of 80 to a Second Grade, First Class Certificate and a percentage of 70 to a Second Class Certificate.

J. M. Simmons, County Commissioner.

_____, Examiner.

A. K. Squire, Examiner. _G. Chairman_

Warren COUNTY, _March 12th_, 188_3_.

* Scholastic, and not calendar years, are meant.

THOMAS OFFICE—E. I. M. MAJOR, PUBLIC PRINTER.

Teaching certificate for top grade teaching awarded to Allensworth
1864

CHAPTER 10

Life held many more spectacular struggles and triumphs for Rev. Allensworth. He served various Baptist churches around Nashville and Louisville and little villages in between. He always seemed to play the part of preacher *and* teacher, with students of all ages.

Late one evening, in a soul-searching quest, he became achingly aware that though the slaves had been let loose physically by the Emancipation Proclamation and the Civil War, they still needed to be free mentally and emotionally. His work as a traveling minister gave him the opportunity to reach large numbers of them. Preaching to those who were often ignorant, poor, superstitious and illiterate gave him the chance to instill, hope in future in some of them. He promised them that knowledge and education would help make them free; that reading was the road to this freedom. He found deep satisfaction in this work.

In this "circuit ministry" however, Rev. Allensworth battled with some of the most challenging situations he had ever faced. He must settle factions among the church congregations, reorganize memberships, pacify hatreds, overcome religious superstitions, rise above injustices and false accusations and endure personal attacks based on envy.

At the same time it brought him one of his greatest blessings. He found Josephine Leavell, his future wife, who he said, "Made the sweetest music to ever come out of an organ." After two years of courtship, they were married on September 20, 1877. The beautiful pale skinned lady from Trenton, Kentucky shared his ideals as well as his desires to impart what truths he knew.

One crisp November day Rev. Allensworth received an urgent call to be pastor of the Baptist church in Bowling Green, Kentucky, about one hundred sixteen miles south of Louisville. He accepted. Allen and Josephine were happy to spend their honeymoon days just being together and working together in this town once known as the Barrens. (Some old timers say it was so named because of the bare expanse of open prairie surrounded by forests. Others feel its Barren River may have had something to do with naming the town.) At any rate, by the time Allen and Josephine got there the name was Bowling Green. It sat calmly above a network of underground chambers that include the famous Mammoth Cave area.

In this beautiful countryside Allen and Josephine, in addition to their ministerial duties, set up informal school systems for black children who had no education. The words of an ancient anonymous theologian could have been Allen's teaching platform: "It's the thirst after more knowledge, that constant longing after more light, which constitutes the difference between man and brute." They could easily have been Allen's own words.

He and Josephine spent the majority of their efforts helping slake the "thirst after knowledge" in those who sought it. They taught the three "R"s to pupils of all ages. Time nibbled away the weekdays in teachings, and the Sundays in preachings like a rhythmic pendulum. One day the General Association of the Colored Baptists in Kentucky called him to conduct their financial affairs.

Again in Louisville, Rev. Allensworth couldn't have dreamed that managing the "financial affairs" of the Association would involve founding a college. It was said to be the "first effort by the enlightened Negroes of Kentucky to establish a self-supporting institution to better the moral and intellectual welfare of {the black} race." In 1880, with Co-founder, William H. Steward, Allensworth and the Association established and incorporated the college and called it The State University.

Both men agreed that Rev. W.J. Simmons, venerable pastor of the Lexington Baptist Church should be their first president. Simmons, knew that reliance solely on the precarious income of often poor students was not a stable occupation. He insisted that Allensworth and Steward guarantee his salary. In a self-sacrificing move, they agreed to pay Simmons' out of their own meager earnings.

Allensworth remained on the Board of Trustees for several years. Rev. Simmons stayed until 1890. Over a hundred and thirteen years later, after many struggles, the school is still in operation, and now bears the name of its first president. The Simmons Bible College in Louisville is today turning out excellent men and women to be of good service to humanity.

•   •   •

Reverend Allensworth's career carried him back and forth across the state, where he served as pastor and educator. Through many successes and hardships, he coped with jealousy and un-Christian conduct, improving conditions wherever he went, establishing new churches and re-organizing memberships. In Louisville he established the Centennial Baptist Church of Louisville, the first Baptist Church in Kentucky to be incorporated, and where the congregation went from 45 to 220 in number. At times he would take no salary except the money from one collection per month. If the amount exceeded $35 he donated the surplus back to the Church. Because he spoke with "firmness and clearness", as one of his listeners said, he was called upon to give lectures now and then.

Despite all his successes, one of the scars of slavery clung to Rev. Allensworth like welts from the beatings he had endured. He still carried an almost sub-conscious burden of mediocrity. Nervous timidity tightened its grip on him whenever he talked to large groups of white people. To help overcome these feelings he, at one time, enrolled in the National School of Elocution and Oratory in Philadelphia. Here he discovered, among his first lessons, how to enunciate carefully, and breathe properly and rid himself of his "Southern brogue".

The standard textbook for teaching the art of speaking, already in its 95th printing by then, was the *Rhetorical Reader* by Ebenezer Porter D.D. Reading aloud excerpts from the Bible and writings of early authors like Washington Irving and John Knox in this little book, the student learned articulation and inflection, gestures and emphasis.

A poem, by William Cowper written in the late 1700's, quoted in Porter's *Reader* and other school books of the times, echoed Allen's views and flavored his speeches. The parts he would remember the most from the longish poem, *The Negro's Complaint*, were:

> Forced from home and all its pleasures
> Africa's coast I left forlorn;
> To increase a stranger's treasures,
> O're the raging billows borne.
> Men from England bought and sold me,
> Paid my price in paltry gold;
> But though slave they have enroll'd me
> *Minds* are never to be sold.

And, farther on:

> Fleecy locks, and black complexion
> Cannot forfeit Nature's claim;
> *Skins* may differ, but *affection*
> Dwells in white and black the same.

The President of the elocution school and the press praised him highly as a public speaker. One report that appeared in the *Boston Watchman* read: "He was born an orator, and so well educated that there is nothing provincial in his accent or pronunciation. The attention of the audience was won at once and the interest sustained throughout."

Another, the *Franklin, Kentucky Favorite* wrote: "His is no ordinary mind, and besides he possesses the happy faculty of knowing how to express himself in the most pleasant and learned style, his reasoning being logical and winning."

Allen could hardly believe they were writing about him. The lack of confidence and distrust of his ability wafted away like pollen on a breezy day. A growing sense of self-assurance freed him from encumbering thoughts that would muddle his message.

Consequently, he signed a contract with the Williams Lecture Bureau in Boston. Invitations to give lectures to colleges and literary societies arrived in quantity. In his deep, mellifluous voice his speeches included quotes from such scholarly personalities as Homer, Demosthenes, Aristotle, Plato, and Nero, showing the wide scope his reading had given him. Though he probably wasn't consciously aware of it, he had reached the "temple of knowledge" uncle Rueben had explained to him from his first little book bought when he was twelve.

The figure his audiences saw on the platform was of a man of stature. Though still jockey-sized, he stood so straight people often thought of him as a tall man. His dignity and bearing gave his communications strength and earned the admiration of his listeners. He had a thin, straight nose and deep, sympathetic eyes that seemed to have tomes of poetry lying hidden behind them waiting to get out. He enjoyed being well dressed on the platform despite the stiff starchy and uncomfortably high collars in fashion in those days. Still, his fine clothing enabled him so to forget himself that he could concentrate on his topics.

A lecture tour throughout New England and the Eastern States spread his message of inspiration. It encouraged audiences of all races and ages to reach for the promise of mastery over self.

Two of these lectures, *The Battle of Life and How to Fight It* , (see Appendix I) and *The Five Manly Virtues* generated high respect. One Franklin, Kentucky newspaper report of his day said of the orator, "Mr. Allensworth is a striking example of what culture can do for the Negro. He possesses fine logical powers, a bright and scintillating wit and a fund of pathos, which is all the more effective because sparingly used." Allensworth's self-confidence blossomed like a sturdy Southern magnolia.

The "Five Manly Virtues" he chose as a subject were Industry, Fidelity, Gentleness, Fortitude and Prudence. At all times he stressed, **"Never Stop Learning"**. Allen could often overhear remarks from his audiences praising his ability as they left the auditorium.

One of these listeners, Delilah Beasley, remembered hearing him speak when she was a child in Cincinnati. She later wrote (in 1919), that the experience of hearing him was one of her sacred memories. "The inspiring lessons derived from his lecture *'Master-*

ing the Situation' have been a guiding star through life", she wrote.[9]

In another lecture Allensworth said, *"There is much latent force both in men and women of which the world knows nothing, simply because the conditions of their lives are such that their strongest gifts remain dormant".* It was this latent, dormant force that Allensworth endeavored to bring out in young people in all his life and work. He would often say, speaking of the heroic side of human nature, *"Of this class, Benjamin Franklin stands almost alone in his ability to overcome adverse circumstances."* Future ages could well say the same about the lecturer.

Elaborating on this ability to overcome adverse circumstances, Allensworth wrote in a black periodical, *"A great deal has been said and written about the causes that operate against our success in competing with the white man for an equal chance in the race of life, but the writers and speakers overlook the fact that we are handicapped by weight that we alone can remove. We are continually complaining of what we call color prejudice and charging our individual failure to that cause, without taking into account existing conditions and facts. It is a <u>condition</u> that we are to deal with and not color; . . . This condition has been brought about by permission of public opinion; all the laws against us are merely public opinion in legal forms. To change these laws we must change public opinion by meeting its demands. . . .What are we to do? Educate public opinion."* For full text. See Appendix I.

Artist's sketch of a preacher and his mixed congregation, typical of Allensworth's experiences.

CHAPTER 11

Reverend Allensworth's high regard kept rising. He commanded respect and favor wherever he went. He amassed a list of
accomplishments and credits that would rival Booker T. Washington.
He earned his credentials that allowed him to teach in the public
schools. A Colored Baptist Sunday School Convention appointed
him State Sunday School Superintendent. All this gave him the
greater opportunity to work with young people. He loved to inspire
them with higher morals and values that he hoped would steer
them through life.

He gained fame as an orator. He became known as a champion
of his race, answering calls from various groups for counseling
when racial questions arose. Life was good. He had a beautiful
wife who stood behind him to help with any situation.

He now realized one of his lifetime dreams: having his mother
come to live with him. And how long old Phyllis had prayed to be
with her son. It lifted her heart beyond her hopes to see the rever-
ence he evoked from blacks and whites alike. Her gratitude at
seeing his place in the world brought peace to the 96 year old lady.
You can almost hear her saying, "Thankie Jesus, Thankie Jesus".
She passed quietly away in 1878. Her son was thirty six.

Allen was heartbroken, of course, but his life was much too
full to spend long hours in despondency. Because of his wide
spread enthusiasms for things cultural and progressive, it wasn't
surprising that he became interested in national politics. His pleas-
ing personality, and by now excellent manner of speaking made
him a likely prospect. He inspired confidence among politicians of
both parties and all races. "The Republican convention of

Kentucky's Third Congressional District twice elected him as a delegate—Kentucky's only black delegate, in both 1880 and 1884."

His career included personal associations with such well known history-book names as Presidents James Garfield and Chester Arthur. In the latter's 1884 campaign in Chicago, against James G. Blaine, Allen made his decision privately as to which candidate he would support. Several times, however, suave operators contacted him in order to sway his convictions and urge his support for their man. These were tests to the honor and manhood Allensworth stood for, but he never sacrificed his sense of what was right.

It was in this election that the term "mugwump" was coined to indicate a Republican, for example, who refused to support the Republican candidate. Two years later, when Allensworth applied for a Chaplain's position in the Army the term was applied to him by an irreverent young reporter for the *Cincinnati Enquirer*. He wrote, "Now a colored mugwump from Kentucky wants to be appointed a Chaplain."

All the Negro delegates, whatever their districts, at this 1884 convention got high praise from the Chicago press. One paper wrote, "All parties will have to acknowledge that the colored delegates have borne themselves like men throughout the exciting contests in the convention. Some of the best speeches were made by colored men, and they have at all times been courteous, polite and attentive to their duties."

Allensworth's exceptional attitude and character helped earn this praise. His associates who heard him voice his philosophy admired him greatly, and were vocal in their appreciation.

"It was Allensworth's firm conviction", one associate said of him,"that without character as a sure foundation, a place and fair reputation among his fellow-citizens could never be gained, whatever the talk of talents, education, culture, and the pretensions to theoretical rights. Confidence and esteem are based on honorable character, and character must be based on honorable principles, honest and industrious habits and devotion to duty. Such is the foundation upon which a worthy human character is built."

For four years Rev. Allensworth served politics *and* Church. He moved from one small-town Kentucky Church to another, including Elizabethtown, Franklin and then back to Louisville. Coincidence took him back to the building originally built for the Ely Normal Institute that had since turned it over to the American Missionary Association. It became his chapel. Allensworth found himself preaching in the same room where he had his first real school experience.

Back in Bowling Green, now with their two daughters Eva and Nella, Reverend Allensworth began reflecting about his responsibility for their future. Some planning was in order. Many evenings he and Josephine sat discussing their future. He felt that staying in Bowling Green would be too limiting on the girls, without the scope and promise he wanted for them.

His life with Josephine was a hymn, with all the melody and harmony of *Abide With Me,* * the loved hymn that she played in their churches. Life with their daughters simply added lilt to the medley. Josephine loved and was loved by all those in their congregations. She became as much a comfort to them as were her husband's sermons. She shared his appointments with loving adaptability. She allowed her husband to make the important decisions, and she was always ready and willing to move on to his next appointment.

Because of his great love for books, Allen naturally favored assignments in cities where there were good libraries, not only for himself but for his daughters. This led him to accept an appointment as minister in the Union Baptist Church in Cincinnati, Ohio. Here he lectured, preached and taught. It was at this time that Delilah Beasley heard the lecture that changed her life.

The move proved fortuitous for this dedicated family. Allen met a man who urged him to apply for a commission as Army chaplain. Before this the chaplains of Negro regiments had, with one exception, all been white officers. (The exception was a Chaplain Plummer who received a dishonorable discharge.

Allensworth learned that the chaplain of the Twenty-fourth Infantry would be retiring soon. He re-joined the Army and sought the job. It wasn't an easy goal to reach. Black Officers were not a known quality in the Army. Rev. Allensworth spent two years of letter writing and contacting various agencies before he was even nominated for the position. By some strange retribution, Mrs. A.P. Starbird (Miss Bett), wife of his first owner, signed one of his many letters of recommendation. (See Appendix III.) Finally, his friend, Senator Joseph E. Brown of Georgia wrote a strong letter directly to the President requesting the appointment. It must have contained an irresistibly convincing plea.

On April 1, 1886, a Democratic President, Grover Cleveland confirmed the appointment of black Allen Allensworth, a Republican as Chaplain in the United States Army. Allen resigned his position as pastor of the Union Baptist Church and at a reception held there in June the congregation presented him with a handsome gold headed cane. He went by train from Cincinnati and *Chaplain* Allensworth reported for duty with the Twenty Fourth Infantry Regiment on July 11, 1886 at Fort Supply, Indian Territory (later Oklahoma).

When Allen's first Chaplain's uniform arrived, with its black cloth coat, braid trim and handsome leather belt we can imagine the surge of momentary pride jockey-sized officer felt. His thought must have turned back to the elation of that happy day when Mrs. Talbot the Quaker lady, had furnished the little slave with his first real suit of clothing. What a long way he had come since then.

If Matthew Brady, the famous photographer of the day, had pictured him at this point, we would see a fine looking, slender man of 44, hair slightly silvering at the temples, a distinguished, stately, erect figure. The years rested on his shoulders as admirably as his trim uniform.

A surprising meeting at this first duty station would definitely flash his memory back to his days on the Starbird's plantation, and the times he and Eddie played with the neighboring Wolfe brothers, Willie and Nat, Jr. Three days after his arrival at Fort Supply he happened to meet the young men. They had entered the Army a few years after the Civil War. The three met in the Officer's Mess Hall and in some kind of vindication, Allensworth found he carried the higher rank of Captain, not to mention the esteemed title of Chaplain while they both held the lower rank of Second Lieutenants! He also carried the scar from the wound they had accidentally inflicted many years ago.

* The hymn by Henry Francis Lyte, also known as "Eventide".

Josephine Leavell Allensworth, 1877

CHAPTER 12

Two months after Chaplain Allensworth reported for duty at Fort Supply, Josephine arrived with Eva and Nella. The eight-room house assigned to them provided a respectable and comfortable home, suitable for the Chaplain's rank. Nella had become a talent on the violin; so with Josephine at the organ, and Eva's crystalline voice, some lovely music wafted across the sparsely shaded lawns of the Post.

Once again, though, the flowers of triumph carried the painful thorns of incompleteness. Captain Allensworth's total satisfactions at being a Chaplain and re-united with his family were marred for a short time. Despite the handsome uniform, his distinctive position, and the governmental decree that all men should be equal, racial prejudice tried to raise its ugly head. Frequent discourtesies showed he was not receiving the respect his rank and dignified bearing should command. Once, on temporary duty out of town, he inquired about a room at a moderate-priced hotel. The clerk refused the stately Captain with the words, "We don't take coloreds."

The day he left Cincinnati for his first post of duty he waited for his train in the railroad station. A woman walked up to the trimly uniformed Captain.

"Porter", she said, "what time does the 8:45 train arrive"?

"At fifteen minutes to nine, Madame", the Chaplain replied without a flicker of reaction.

Again, at his garrison some of the white soldiers vowed they would never salute a Negro officer. Many of the these men came from the deep South and still held to their beliefs that "colored" men were slave material. Failure to salute a superior officer was an offence that could result in court martial if the officer decided to bring charges. The Chaplain refused to resort to such harshness. Instead, he handled matters in his own humane way.

One day a soldier purposely passed him by without saluting. Chaplain Allensworth called the boy to "attention" and started a general conversation with him. Questions such as "How is your regiment? Your service? Your family?" Carrying on in a casually friendly manner he asked, "Do you write to your mother, soldier? I urge you to not forget her. Write to her regularly". And so the conversation went, until the Chaplain turned around and walked away. Those standing by thought surely, the Officer would call the soldier down. In every case the Chaplain refused to react. To a man, all eventually recognized Captain Allensworth's place and accepted him as an Officer in the United States Army, salute and all.

•   •   •

Pages on the calendar peeled off like the skins of an onion until they became years, and then decades. Captain Allensworth's Chaplaincy included transfers to numbers of challenging duty stations. Many of these were surrounded by Indians. Speaking of Army life in Indian Territory one newspaper writer said, "In the period after the Civil War, one mission of the Army was to give protection to white settlers that were thronging West. At least 1,067 separate engagements were fought against Indian nations. Although the Southern Indians were not attacking as were the Cheyenne and Sioux, the Army's policy was to constantly harass and chase the

Indians to keep them in a state of subjection.

"Generally while the (Fifth) Cavalry was out chasing Indians, the Infantry performed scouting duties and . . . guarded stations, in addition to providing escort for army pay masters, government supply trains and railroad and wagon road construction crews. Fortunately for the Chaplain, his duties did not include combat, but ministering to the spiritual needs of the Posts, to help them fight the 'battle of life'." The article would indicate that the writer was familiar with Allensworth's powerful speech, *The Battle of Life and How to Fight It*". (See Appendix I)

At Fort Bayard, New Mexico in 1888, Chaplain Allensworth's "chapel" was a sparsely furnished room with chairs from another building borrowed for the Sabbath. The Chaplain managed to have enough chairs ordered in, so all could be seated while listening to his illustrated sermons. Here he introduced the use of the stereopticon, a novel idea for pastors, and delivered sermons on such themes as "Pilgrim's Progress".

He found time to write an article on the "Social Status of the Race" for *The New York Age* . (See Appendix II). Referring again to his theme that it was "<u>conditions</u> that should be dealt with instead of color", he wrote in part, "We do not realize, as fully as we should, that we hold to many false ideas and practices in social life, that militate against us more than any other sociological factor"; and "We must keep the education of the home up to that of the school house, that we may be able to enforce at home the rules of decency and morality, the laws of pure and safe homes the world over. . . We must improve our social status, we must have social distinctions; we must draw a line between the refined and unrefined."

Other duty stations after Fort Sill, included Fort Douglas, Salt Lake City, Utah; Fort Harrison, Montana; Fort Huachuca, Arizona; the Philippines, and Fort McDowell in San Francisco. On June 17, 1904 at one of these duty stations he was promoted to the rank of Major because of his "exceptional efficiency."

A Chaplain's duties at Army posts often included such unspiritual responsibilities as post treasurer, post librarian and overseer of garden supplies. Nearest Allensworth's heart, after preaching was serving as Superintendent of Post schools. This meant setting up entire school systems on the base. He wrote a manual for a course of study for both children and soldiers. The first grade was for Privates, the second for Corporals, third for Sergeants, and so on. Here was the man who, as a youth, ached so much even to learn the *basics* of reading that he endured whippings for it, and now he was *writing the textbooks* for others!

Allensworth's manual was reprinted many times for other Army Posts. Company commanders requested their men to enroll in the courses that qualified the soldiers for better and higher duties. It became a staple in his own teaching wherever he went, and was recommended for general use to the public. In the Chaplain's teaching position he must have inspired his men often with the promise from his *Lindley Murray Reader*, "The acquisition of knowledge is one of the most honorable occupations of youth".

In whatever he could find of spare time, Rev. Allensworth wrote articles of an inspirational nature for magazines. On the basis of his manual and other writings, the National Educational Association invited him to be its regional director and manager. This was some time between the years of 1888 and 1890. He was the only Negro until then to be so honored.

In the summer of 1893 Chaplain Allensworth had the honor of attending the World's Parliament of Religion and the Brotherhood of Christian Unity at the Columbian Exposition in Chicago. A letter of recommendation to the Director-General of the Exposition concerning Allensworth's admission shows, in part, the esteem in which the Chaplain was held.

Fort Bayard, N.M., August 22, 1892

To the Director-General,

World's Columbian Exposition,

Chicago, Illinois

Dear Sir:

Having been informed by Chaplain Allen Allensworth, 24th infantry, of his intention to apply to you as an Army colored man, I take great pleasure in recommending him to your favorable consideration. I have known him since July, 1886, the time he joined the regiment, since that time he has by his industry, faithfulness to duty, interest in the advance of his people, loyalty to the service, and prudence, won the respect and esteem of every officer with whom he has served.

Should you desire his services, as sought by him, you will find him prompt and true, faithful and conservative in the discharge of all duties imposed upon him. His administrative and executive ability is of high order, and business qualities good. He is thoroughly prepared, by knowledge and experience, to represent his people in the Exposition management.

(signed) J. Milton Thompson, Captain,

24th Infantry

Granted temporary leave from his Army post, he took an active and significant part in the event. The meeting was said, at the time, to be one of the greatest influences exerted upon public opinion with a view to reducing race prejudice. No other representative of his race participated except Frederick Douglass who attended on behalf of the Republic of Haiti to dedicate the Haitian Pavilion.

Douglass spoke at a special "Colored People's Day" at this Fair. In his usual powerful voice he said, "Men talk of the Negro problem. There is no Negro problem. The problem is whether the American people have loyalty enough to live up to their own Constitution,." He, with Allensworth, hoped that all people would also live by Thomas Jefferson's words in the Declaration of Independence that "All Men are created equal, that they are endowed by their Creator with certain unalienable Rights, that among these are Life, Liberty, and the Pursuit of Happiness".

With the Exposition over, Allensworth, the man of wide and varied interests took advantage of his stay in Chicago for yet another learning experience. He read of a cooking course, "The Science of Cooking" given by the Armour Institute. He explained to his Army superiors that the course would "form a valuable supplement to the Manual of Cooking furnished by the Subsistence Department." He received special permission to stay over. Being the ready learner that he had become, he finished the one year course in three months, and returned to his next duty station.

CHAPTER 13

Chaplain Allensworth arrived at Fort Douglas, three miles from Salt Lake City, in October of 1896. It was the year Utah became the forty-fifth state of the Union, and William McKinley got elected as the twenty-fifth President of the United States.

The entrance of the Twenty Fourth Infantry into the Fort Douglas area riled the residents to an unwelcoming pitch. The all black Twenty Fourth regiment replaced an all white Sixteenth Infantry. The townspeople had enjoyed the soldiers of the Sixteenth and definitely did not want the black soldiers. They were convinced that there would be drunken carousings and trouble on the street cars. They feared a general immoral atmosphere surrounding the black soldiers.

But they were reckoning without Chaplain Allensworth. His teachings, his sermons and his example had sufficiently inspired his men to a life of morality. He informed a local newspaper, the *Broad Ax*, that he "would be more than pleased if all the saloons, gambling houses and immoral houses would absolutely refuse to entertain the Negro soldiers."

He felt the utmost confidence in their moral strength and behavior. After settling into Fort Douglas life Allensworth left the regiment for a short span of temporary duty at Fort Huachuca, Arizona. The Fort had no Chaplain of its own so Allensworth filled in the gap until one could be appointed.

Though he was only there a short time, an official report said of him, on his return to Utah,

"While at Fort Huachuca [Chaplain Allensworth] conducted religious instruction, delivered a series of educational lectures, and organized a literary society. The men were greatly benefited and inspired by the service rendered. This is another evidence of the Chaplain's splendid usefulness in this field of labor."

(Signed, John B. Sanford, lst Lieut. & Batt.
Adjt 24th Inf.)

By the time the Chaplain returned to Fort Douglas, his men had proven their praiseworthy example for the townspeople. They exhibited their ability to uphold his principles, even in their Chaplain's absence. At all social and military happenings Allensworth himself was afforded his proper place at the officers' table and in receiving lines.

When the Twenty-fourth Regiment received their next orders it was to Cuba and the Spanish American War. Their leaving was a totally different picture from the reception they received. Almost the entire city around Fort Douglas came out to bid them farewell—a startling contrast to the near-hostility of their arrival in town.

One editorial in a local newspaper said, "Sad was the day when the [Twenty Fourth] Regiment left Salt Lake".

Another report, written after their departure said of their conduct during their stay at Fort Douglas, " Desertion and alcoholism were low—a sign of well-disciplined troops. The black units met their enemies without faltering, whether against the Indians, the elements, the isolation or racial prejudice and discrimination. While doing so, they compiled a record of achievement of the highest order. Although many of these achievements have been ignored. . . it is important that they never escape further attention".

It went on to credit the success to the outstanding role of the Chaplain.

The Salt Lake Tribune reported when the Regiment left, "The element of color seemed entirely eliminated." Again Chaplain Allensworth had triumphed over the adversity of racial differences.

●   ●   ●

The efforts to save Cuba from oppression by Spain in 1898 brought war clouds again over the United States. The mysterious sinking of the United States battleship *Maine* in Havana harbor on February 15, set off the signal. President McKinley ordered U.S. troops to Cuba. The crack Twenty-Fourth Infantry was among the first to go. The Regiment went without Chaplain Allensworth, however. His Commanding Officers considered him too valuable as a recruiter of much needed men to send into battle. Instead, he went to the Southern states to sign up black troops.

Before his Regiment left, Chaplain Allensworth prepared his men for battle with a memorable speech. They assembled on the Fort Douglas parade ground just ten days after Easter. April skies promised approaching showers but the Regimental band played on with its familiar stirring marches.

Chaplain Allensworth, in full uniform, sat grandly in the saddle of a well-groomed horse that pranced to center front. The strains of *Stars and Stripes Forever* faded courteously as the Chaplain took his place facing the Regiment. The men stood stiffly at attention. Their Chaplain delivered a talk then that the men would remember forever.

"Soldiers and Comrades," he said eloquently, "fate has turned the war dogs loose and you have been called to the front to avenge an insult to our country's flag." (Many people blamed Spain for the loss of the *Maine* and the 260 men aboard.) "Before leaving this lovely home, leaving family and friends behind, I will say to you, 'Quit yourselves like men and fight'. *[Act manly.]* "Keep in mind that the eyes of the world will be upon you and expect great things of you. . . Therefore I say, 'Quit yourselves like men and fight". (Partial text.) *The Bible, Samuel 4:9 , also I Corinthians l6:13). According to a modern translation: Be alert, stand firm in the faith, be brave, be strong).*

After this farewell, the Chaplain embarked on his recruiting mission in Alabama, Tennessee, Louisiana and his home state of Kentucky. He focused his campaign on college students at Universities like Tuskegee and Fisk. He put up many posters around cities, advertising for soldiers. At first he met with strong feelings against enlistment. No funds for advertising came from the War Department so he had to devise his own clever methods. Whenever there was a parade in the towns he would hire a covered wagon, and place fife and drum players inside. This drew attention to the placards on the outside that read,

An Excursion to Cuba
For Young, Unmarried, Negro Men,
Fare And Lunch Furnished Free.
For information apply to 260 Center Street.

The lure brought in many men curious about a free trip to Cuba. When the numbers of recruits lagged he tried another scheme. He placed an advertisement in the local paper saying:

Wanted immediately,
ten young Negro men for the National Police Force;
uniform and equipment furnished free.
For information apply to 260 Center Street."

He would then explain that the National Police Force was the

United States Army and they would be given employment for three years.

He contacted railroad stations, obtaining free transportation into towns. He gave enticing lectures and sermons to young men in churches. Soon he had the pick of the very best. The Chaplain had very high standards for those he recruited, and held to them. He turned down two otherwise likely prospects because they had tattoos of naked women on their arms.

He filled his quota successfully, enlisting 456 soldiers from Kentucky alone. These men fought with the famous Twenty Fourth Regiment for San Juan Hill and immortalized themselves in ten weeks of bloody but triumphant battles. Theodore Roosevelt is credited with calling this ordeal "A splendid little war." (Note: According to most accurate reports the phrase actually came into being in a letter to then colonel Theodore Roosevelt from United States Ambassador to England, John Hay.) Details of the victorious events that brought Cuba under United States rule, while sometimes controversial, can be found in the pages of most history books.

Official records show that the soldiers in this black regiment took to heart the Fort Douglas farewell message from their Chaplain to "act like men." They were lauded and appreciated from many directions. Several books have been written about their accomplishments.

One authority calls the Twenty Fourth Infantry "the Army's best black regiment". A captain in one of the volunteer regiments who witnessed the battles said, "The Twenty Fourth did more than any other to win the day at San Juan".

After the victory in Cuba, both Allensworth and his Regiment returned to Fort Douglas. On their arrival back at the Utah post, the bone-tired, war weary men marched to their quarters. The regimental band welcomed them with Sousa-like marches which lifted their spirits a hair's breadth. Banners that swung across the streets, celebrated their valor in huge print saying :

**"A Hundred Thousand Welcomes to
the Heroes of San Juan"**

and

"You Have Quit Yourselves Like Men"

Ironically, this battle sent many blacks into the fray who had fought similarly for their *own* rights in the Civil War.

Allensworth was happy to have his men back and to be their Chaplain again. The stay at Fort Douglas was disappointingly brief, however, because as history also records, the fight for Philippine independence from Spain further involved the United States. The Regiment received orders to proceed to Manila by way of Fort McDowell, Angel Island, San Francisco from which they would sail. A tearful separation left Josephine and the two girls situated in beautiful quarters in the fog-cleansed city by the Golden Gate where they would await the Chaplain's return.

Always the helpful Army wife Josephine walked right through any slights that might arise racially or socially. She devoted herself to the support of her husband and his work. The girls' friends were naturally children of other officers because of their father's rank. Josephine trained them well in the life on Army bases. She was always on call to help wives of the enlisted men.

Reverend Allensworth boarded the steamship *"City of Para"*, and sailed out the Golden Gate, across the Pacific Ocean toward Manila. The trip afforded him a degree of leisure and even luxury, both as rare as diamonds in his life. A three day stop in Honolulu gave him and the troops a friendly welcome from the townspeople. Attractive brown skinned natives placed fragrant leis around the soldiers' necks. There were new and delicious fruits to taste. Many of the Hawaiians carried silk banners saying "Aloha Nui to Our Boys in Blue".

'This luxury of free time allowed Allensworth a chance to reflect on his past performance as an Army Officer. As the steamship roiled a huge wake in the blue waters, Chaplain Allensworth might have looked back on the richness of his experiences at his various duty stations. Wherever he served he had always tried to leave the situation in some way better than he found it. He could look back on such instances as:

• At Fort Bayard, New Mexico he had discovered there wasn't a semblance of a church. He found no organ, and no place for his sermons but one small utility room. Even so, it must have quickened his soul to remember that attendance had swelled to a congregation of one hundred and forty-six parishioners. He had formed a literary and debating society at this post. His educational work was so outstanding that it was here the National Education Association caught up with him, and asked for his services .

His Commanding General at Fort Bayard wrote:

"I am glad to commend the excellent service rendered by Chaplain Allensworth, Twenty Fourth Infantry, whose intelligent and earnest efforts are accomplishing most satisfactory results in his Regiment."

Signed,
Frank Wheaton, Brigadier General,
Commanding

Allensworth made sure the Chaplain following him had a suitable place in which to preach his sermons.

• On his short tour of duty at Fort Harrison, Montana, again he had no chapel in which to preach his sermons. Josephine, Eva and Nella had helped apply some of the little comforts that would make the allotted space more homey and welcoming. A little paint, cretonne covering for the chairs and lace curtains spread a cheerful atmosphere over the dingy room. It was here at Fort Bayard that he introduced the use of the stereopticon as a teaching aid which met with much success. He formed the thriving Christian Endeavor Society, including support from the city people.

• He could feel satisfied that he had left established, well-founded educational systems at each post, which would remain open to black and white soldiers and their families.

• And though he would probably not be dwelling on the point as the *City of Para* sped toward its dreaded destination, the textbook he later wrote for education at Army Posts had been reprinted for general use throughout the Army. Company Commanders requested their men to enroll in the courses, which in turn qualified the soldiers for better and higher duties.

In his reveries Chaplain Allensworth might even have mused briefly over the coincidence of Aprils in his life:

      —Born April 7, 1842;

      —first ran away on an April day;

      — saw the Civil War start in April, 1861

      —joined the Navy on April 4, 1863; served until
          April 1865.

      —ordained as Minister by Baptist Church April 9,
          1871.

      —Grover Cleveland signed his appointment as
          Chaplain April 1, 1886;

      —Pres. McKinley issued the order that started the
          Spanish American War, and on April 20, 1898

Allensworth went South to recruit men for Cuba and the Philippines.

(And though he couldn't have foreseen it as the ship neared the Philippines, he and his family would narrowly miss the Great (April 18) 1906 Earthquake that destroyed so much of the city of San Francisco across the Bay from their Angel Island Fort.

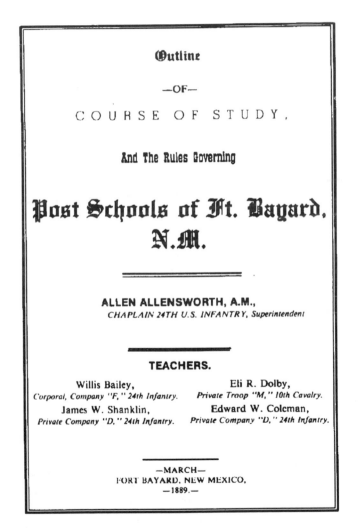

Cover of the Training Manual written by Chaplain Allensworth at Fort Bayard, New Mexico

OATH OF OFFICE.

One to accompany the acceptance of every commissioned officer appointed or commissioned by the President in the Army of the United States.

I, _Allen Allensworth_ , having been appointed a _Chaplain_
in the military service of the United States, do solemnly swear (or affirm) that I will support and defend the Constitution of the United States against all enemies, foreign and domestic, that I will bear true faith and allegiance to the same; that I take this obligation freely, without any mental reservation or purpose of evasion; and that I will well and faithfully discharge the duties of the office on which I am about to enter. So help me God.

Allen Allensworth.
Chaplain 24th Infantry.

Sworn to and subscribed before me, at _Cincinnati_
Ohio , this _30th_ day of _April_ , 1886.

Vincent A. Schmrat
Justice of the Peace

Oath of Office on being promoted to rank of Chaplain.

CHAPTER 14

As his troop ship sailed into Manila harbor Allensworth at once admired the scenic Capitol city. He could see on the hillsides the growing plantain and the peanut vines. The symmetry of terraced rice paddies amid bamboo huts. He reveled in the beauty of lush and verdant tropical growth covering the countryside.

Once on land, however, the picture darkened. Intense heat broiled the camps between punishing rains. Disease and lack of food and medicine made his job as Chaplain intense. In contrast he witnessed striking evidences of heroism, gallantry and self sacrifice among his men. These instances couldn't dispell the gloom hovering over his pressing duties. Nor could they offset working conditions in the city. Traffic patterns on the streets were unrestrained, and undisciplined.

One steamy day, after a particularly harrowing morning ministering to wounded soldiers, the Chaplain met with an accident. The horse drawing his carriage bolted and ran amok. The Chaplain received a serious injury to his knee. The painful wound resisted treatment. Without his dear wife's care Allensworth became physically sick and over-worked. After suffering as long as he could, he reluctantly requested a leave of absence.

Part of the problem that ailed the conscientious Chaplain may have been his heart-sickness on viewing the ghastly conditions of the battlefields. It would have deeply touched the heart of the strongest officer to see his black soldiers, many of them ex-slaves, here in the Philippines, giving their lives to suppress an unknown enemy, so the Filipinos could win *their* fight for freedom.

His commanding officer granted his request for leave. He left the Philippines with high commendation and praise. Many sources acknowledged his service as diligent, energetic, valuable, faithful, and a source of comfort to the soldiers. One such accolade came from J.M. Thompson, who, years before, as a *Captain* (J. Milton Thompson) wrote a letter of recommendation concerning Allensworth's appointment as representative to the Columbian Exposition. By this time a retired Brigadier General, Thompson's letter reads:

> To Chaplain Allen Allensworth,
>
> 24th U.S. Infantry
>
> Referring to your service in the Army, I desire to go on record as saying that I consider you the most all round efficient Chaplain I have known in the Army during my entire service.
>
> For years you have retained the respect of officers and men with whom you have been associated. You have at all times worked for the improvement of your regiment and the service.
>
> In educational matters at Posts you have always been in the lead, and your influence over men in discipline and conduct has ever been for the best.
>
> I especially wish to refer to your efficiency in the field during active operations in the Philippines in 1899, 1900 and 1901 when your hard work was of great benefit to officers and men.
>
> Sincerely yours,
>
> (Signed) J.M. Thompson
>
> Brigadier General, U.S. Army, Ret.

His request for a leave of absence granted in good grace, Allensworth returned to Fort McDowell the post he most enjoyed. It was another long ocean voyage. This time he had a stop over in Japan. Despite the pain remaining from his unfortunate Philippine experiences Chaplain Allensworth was as happy as he had ever been. Stationed at Fort McDowell on the aptly named Angel Island he could again be with his wife and daughters. This brought the weary Chaplain contentment and "the peace of God which passeth all understanding". *(Philippians 4:07)* He recovered just sufficiently to resume his duties as Chaplain.

This picturesque Island Fort rested serenely on the waters of San Francisco Bay. Native oaks and manzanita trees dot the mountainsides. It offered a 360 degree view of the Bay Area.

It also offered the aging Chaplain a period of recuperative rest in between his Chaplain's duties. In moments of quiet he could look back on a long list of social and racial triumphs dealing with his fellow man. Always, one of his foremost duties to the soldiers was to be their friend. He enjoyed sharing some of these contacts with Josephine and his daughters.

One such instance he told her about occurred when the Post hospital called him for help.

"Chaplain, we have a soldier here we can't do anything with", the Army doctor told him.

The young Private was overcome with fear, over-worked physically and mentally, and had tried to commit suicide. He had lain in the hospital bed for days without speaking. The Chaplain spent well over an hour talking to the soldier but received not the slightest response. Not even a nod. About to give up and leave the room, as a last resort, the Chaplain was led to say the only words that the man had responded to for days.

"Soldier, do you have any friends?" the concerned Chaplain asked.

"No sir", the man answered weakly.

"Then I will be your friend, and you can have anything you want as soon as you get off the sick list", the Chaplain promised. The man quickly rallied, and was honorably discharged because of his disability. In today's language this was an early example of "friend therapy."

The soldier would never forget his loving friend, any more than the Chaplain could forget the emotional incident.

Rejuvenated by the wholesome atmosphere and nourished by his family's loving care, Allensworth's life at Angel Island moved along as normally as the tide that lapped the island's edges. But, like the tide, it was still not without the flotsam of occasional racial rubble. Many of the soldiers here at this all white garrison hadn't had much experience with black officers, or black neighbors for that matter. Even some of the high ranking officers weren't sure they wanted to live next door to a Black family.

"I have discovered that he is a cultured gentleman," one white Major said, "yet I am afraid to call on him because of what other people will think and say; while at the same time I am associating on intimate terms with some white men whom I loathe."

But with amiable, and charming grace, the Allensworths overcame the petty prejudices directed at them and became an integral part of social life on the Island and at the Presidio of San Francisco across the Bay.

Even so, the jetsam of discrimination floated just beneath the surface causing undue insecurities. What might have been an uncomfortable situation arose when a young white officer and his fiancee asked the Chaplain if he would perform their wedding ceremony. It was an unusual request for a Black Chaplain, but of course Allensworth agreed to do it. He told Mrs. Allensworth the plan.

"The girl's mother will never allow it. She's a Southern born woman." Josephine told him.

But the plans progressed normally. A large hall was elaborately decorated with red, white and blue bunting. There were flags, crossed muskets and all the fittings proper for a full military event. This included an extravagant dinner-reception after the ceremony.

A few days before the wedding some of the neighbor children were discussing the affair with the Allensworth girls, Nella and Eva.

"Are you and your parents going to sit down to dinner with the wedding party?" [all white] one of the playmates asked.

When the girls told their father about the conversation, it was a blow that hit the Chaplain as forcefully as from a brass-knuckled fist. He suddenly realized what that would mean to some of the men and women of the garrison. He and Josephine discussed it seriously. As always his consideration was for others, in this case the father and mother of the bride. Allen decided to perform the ceremony, mingle with the guests for a short while and then depart, without attending the banquet.

After the vows were said, dinner was announced. The stately Chaplain bowed his farewell to the hostess, claiming another engagement. That might have been the end of the matter, but a few days later the bride's mother came to call on the Allensworths.

"I am sorry that you were not at the supper," she told the couple. Allensworth, inwardly surprised at the remark, explained that he was aware of the racial feelings of some of the guests and did not want to arouse ill feelings.

"That was a wise and gentlemanly thing to do", she told them. "I may be from the South, but I'm not a snob. As a matter of fact, it was I who suggested the young people ask you to marry them." The whole event spread an even greater aura of respect over the Allensworth family, and they entered graciously into the give and take of military social life.

The few years on this island garrison included handsome living quarters in a protected cove, where fresh, invigorating breezes blew over them often enough to keep the climate perfect. From the top of the hills they could see straight out the Golden Gate.

The Chaplain had his own real chapel in which to preach his sermons. It still stands in crisp whiteness, in a toyon-studded valley. Its traditional steeple symbolically reaches toward the sky It was a luxurious contrast to so many of the other military bases where he had used whatever make-shift building could be found for his religious instruction. Fort McDowell seemed to the Allensworths the most pleasant geographical assignment they'd had. It was no wonder that Chaplain Allensworth would think of California first when it came time for retirement.

Military policy orders the issue of an Efficiency Report on all service people annually. Chaplain Allensworth's Report on June 30, 1901 at Fort McDowell read:

- Capacity for command: Excellent;
- Professional zeal: Excellent;
- Conduct and habits: Excellent;
- Condition of men: Excellent,

and so it went. It was standard fare for the Chaplain.

Today, Allensworth's adventures, battles, experiences as the religious adviser to soldiers, black and white, Protestant and Catholic, tolerant and prejudiced, remain unacknowledged except by the United States Army records. His military superiors could not resist recognizing the strength of character, nobility, integrity, humility and patience he exhibited. His genuine love for God and his fellow man helped him overcome all the obstacles. Josephine, whom he referred to as "my better two-thirds", suffered with him equally in the indignities and rejoiced with him at his triumphs.

The Chaplain's wife had exemplary qualities which were also never acknowledged. She earned but never received equal billing for her moral support of her husband. There are no efficiency reports for Officers' wives. Yet she was the behind -the-scenes heroine in some of her husband's most trying situations. It meant assurance and confidence for him to know she was so capably raising Eva and Nella and caring for their homes wherever they went. When the Chaplain went to the Philippines she laboriously kept all his books and records as efficiently as he could have done them himself. She acted as treasurer for enlisted men's wives when their allotment checks came in.

Throughout their marriage she played charming hostess to the members of his churches. With their musical talents she and their daughters supplied excellent music and entertainment at parties. On Army posts she was a gracious and compassionate "Chaplain's lady".

●　　　　●　　　　●

In 1897, the Grand Army of the Republic invited Col. Allensworth to deliver an oration. (*The Grand Army of the Republic was an organization of Union Veterans of the Civil War, started in April 1866 to preserve friendships, honor fallen soldiers and aid their widows.)* In his speech Allensworth characterized Abraham Lincoln, in part thusly:

"He was one of those grand and stalwart characters that amid a million gleaming lights outshines and attracts them all. Without assumption or conceit the honors which he achieved and all that were bestowed upon him became his quiet grace and dignity. His character was independent, strong and self-reliant. His perceptions were keen, his judgment cool, his course direct, his arguments convincing. Not before his sudden and tragic end was his great worth realized."

Those who knew Allensworth might have later said the same about him.

Chaplain Allensworth once told a friend his aim throughout his military service "was to prove to the world that a Negro could be an officer and a gentleman; and further to educate the Negro soldier up to the point where he could prove himself a man and a soldier, to educate Caucasians to the point of recognizing that a Negro possesses sufficient manly virtues to comply with all of the conditions required by the Army regulation and military customs."

There is no doubt that he was successful in his aims to "educate the Negro." He received nation-wide recognition for his "expertise in education". Word spread as far across the country as the Baptist Roger Williams University in Nashville, Tennessee where he had studied. The school awarded him an honorary Master of Arts degree in 1887. *(This college, no longer in existence, is not to be confused with the existing Roger Williams University in Bristol, Rhode Island).*

The masterful way he handled the striking incidences of racial prejudice show his own proof that a Negro could be an "officer and a gentleman" with all the social graces that go with these qualities.

By his own example he proved that "a Negro possess sufficient manly virtues to comply with all of the conditions required by the Army regulation and military customs". The reams of accolades from Commanding Officers throughout his career attest to his success on that score.

The Chaplain's aim to "educate Caucasians to the point of recognizing that a Negro possesses sufficient qualities. . ." perhaps has as yet to be realized by the world. In his own case, with all his extraordinary accomplishments, if his name can be found in any encyclopedia he's often merely listed as a jockey! (Remember, back in Louisville, as a slave in Fred Scruggs stables?)

And, yes, he did get to Canada! Freedom came years before, but he never forgot the slave-dream he thought would set him free. The *actuality* of the dream came in a way he could never have imagined. The National Education Association, of which he was still regional manager, invited him to present a paper at it's annual convention in Toronto in 1891.

As a Chaplain on leave from the Army, he explained to Josephine, he had to pay his own expenses and go on his own time due to War Department regulations. On his arrival, he decided it was well worth the cost. Here he was, in a position of honor and FREE; free as an eagle in morning's light. No longer shackled to fear as in his slave days. Looking back on those early dreams and comparing them with his present circumstances he must have used his mother's prayer, "Thankie Jesus, thankie God".

●   ●   ●

The years ambled along and soon became 1906. George Bernard Shaw's plays were huge hits in New York; the great San Francisco earthquake would kill 400 people and endanger the life of Enrico Caruso, famed tenor. In April of that year, Chaplain Allensworth had served twenty years in government service (including his Naval duty). Because he was still suffering from the injuries he experienced in Manila, he chose to retire on April 7. He was promoted to the prestigious rank of Lieutenant Colonel. The trail-blazing responsibility of being the first black man to receive this rank seemed a natural addition to his known abilities.

The Cleveland (Ohio) *Gazette* for April 21 reported it as "the highest honor ever given an Afro-American in the Army". He received multitudes of letters of congratulations, and high praises. The Twenty-Fourth Infantry presented the family with a large silver tray and silver candelabra. Many of his early lectures published in newspapers were still widely circulating. Several people urged him to write his life story to inspire others. A few years hence he would begin relating and dictating his memoirs to a learned, esteemed writer, Charles Alexander when fate put an abrupt halt to the project.

Officers quarters on Angel Island where Josephine, Eva and Nella waited
for Allensworth while he was in the Philipines

CHAPTER 15

In June, following his retirement, Col. Allensworth moved with his family to Los Angeles, California. His thoughts were filled with finding how he could further serve his race. He had observed during his stay at Fort McDowell in Northern California that the mental climate was more open and accepting to Blacks in the Golden State. This was only partially true in Southern California, he was to find. Even though they were free souls, many Blacks still found it almost impossible to get good jobs. Few could own their own homes, and not many were educated.

For a long time Allensworth had dreamed of an all Black town, run by its own people. It would be a place where they could own property and be responsible for its city government. His attention soon centered on the rich farmland of central California's San Joaquin Valley. He felt he could start such a township here in the flat and fertile land, about halfway between San Francisco and Los Angeles. It was in Tulare County twenty-five miles from the nearest large city, Bakersfield.

With his young friend, William Payne, also an ex-slave and a highly regarded Black teacher, they founded a small community. It was 1909, the year Henry Ford produced the Model T Ford (priced at $850, later reduced to $290) and one year after boxer Jack Johnson became the first black heavyweight champion of the world. The town had many good things going for it. Three essentials were already established: the railroad, plenty of water and good farm land. To honor its founder the people named it Allensworth.

Soon the town spread over several hundred acres, if you included the farm land. Among the first buildings was, logically, the school. Professor Payne was its first Principal. Soon there were stores, a hotel, blacksmith shop and Post Office. And of course a church, school district and *a library*. In a gesture as natural as breathing, Col. Allensworth gave the contents of his own large book collection to the library. Mrs. Allensworth, first lady of the town, established a women's club, brass band, and a glee club. The people raised their own food and sold what they didn't need. The largest crops were cotton, alfalfa and sugar beets. Cows and rabbits mingled with various pet dogs in the pastures.

By 1914 the town consisted of a group of "aspiring, self-respecting, self supporting, self-governing, cooperative townsfolk." All Black. Delilah Beasley, author of *Negro Trail Blazers* says of them, "They were not only settlers, but pioneers in spirit and deeds, willing to toil and hustle for development." Through their efforts the settlement became a market center for the valley.

Col. Allensworth went back to Southern California to promote the growing community. Here, he would tell them, a man could afford to own his own farm. He could grow his own crops and reap the profit for himself. He would be living among his own people. Even the school teachers would be of the same race.

In Monrovia (near Los Angeles) one hot September Sunday in 1914 he was on his way to give a sermon. He stepped off a Pacific Electric street car when a speeding motorcycle whizzed by, striking down the 72 year old gentleman. The accident was fatal.

He was buried with full military honors and surrounded by hundreds of friends and admirers. Memorial services to honor the extraordinary Black Chaplain were held all over the state and other parts of the country. It should be written on his tombstone: *He was a man of quiet grace, who talked with God while he walked among men.*

Afro-American history still trembles in the winds of change. Growing numbers of serious thinkers feel such role models as Allen Allensworth will bring the time when judging character will be done on the basis of real charity as Webster (Second, Unabridged) defines it, "the disposition to love all men as brothers because they are sons of God"; when worth will be judged by motives and deeds and not skin color or racial origin.

In one of his major speeches, considering the characters that have made history, Col. Allensworth said *"Not all life's battles are fought in the bloody chasm, nor on fields red with gore; neither have all its victories been won by an Alexander, a Nero, Napoleon, Grant or Sheridan. In the humbler walks of life have been found men and women who have done grander deeds and won more enduring laurels. Their deeds may not have been published in newspapers, nor their names embalmed in libraries. Fame has refused to herald them abroad, obscure and unknown they have acted their part in the drama of life and have passed on; but if we mistake not, a record of their deeds will be found in the book of life".* Little could he have known that these words could be used to describe his own life.

The town of Allensworth, the Afro-American race and the nation lost a hero, a valued citizen when Col. Allensworth passed on. But their honorable leader bequeathed to them an extraordinary example. By believing the promise that the path to freedom was through learning, he truly came out of the darkness into the light.

The End

30PO.R 36 Gort.

Los-Angeles,California; Sept.;16th-1914

Adjutant General Army

Washington; DC .

I report that Allen Allensworth Chaplain retired was struck
by a motor-cycle at Monrovia California thirteenth instant and died from
injuries at Ten P:M. fourteenth instant at Monrovia .

Hubbard Chaplain Retired'.

3:30-P:M.   Received A.G.U., SEP 10 ...

Telegram announcing the death of Allensworth.

Allensworth's Chapel on Angel Island as it stands today.
(Courtesy of John Soennichsen)

AFTERWORD

Colonel Allensworth had great hopes and plans for his new settlement. On June 27, 1908 he wrote to his hero, Booker T. Washington telling of the proposed city:

"I have secured over nine thousand acres of the richest land in Central California where the Colony will be located on the main line of the Santa Fe railroad. A town will be established upon the most scientific basis and improved methods of city building.

" We intend to . . .encourage our people to develop the best there is in them under the most favorable conditions of mind and body.

"It is my desire to have our streets given names of historical and educational value. In the midst of this city we will have a lake, surrounded by a park, to be named—if you have no objection—'Washington' park, in honor of the greatest Negro sentiment maker in the world. Have you any objection?
Respectfully yours, Allen Allensworth. Lieut-Colonel U.S.A. Retired.

Washington had no objections, but destiny had other plans.

For a time the town did prosper and grew to a population of several hundred. On Saturdays the brass band marched through the dusty streets. The debating society met once a month. Crops thrived and many people earned a satisfactory living. It had its own justice of the peace, and many civic minded citizens. One of its early residents, Gemelia Herring now in her late 80's, says "I thought Allensworth was one of the most beautiful places I ever saw. The grass was always green and wild flowers grew all over."

The town struggled along without its leader from the time of the Colonel's death until the Nineteen Thirties. Gradually change began to eat away all that had given the town life. The Santa Fe Railroad built a spur track to nearby Alpaugh and deprived the town of any commercial stops. It was a threatening blow to the life-blood of the farming community.

A few years later, the farmers sadly discovered the water to be full of salt, so the crops wouldn't grow. The Great Depression was on and towns-people couldn't find jobs. Before long the population dwindled and Allensworth became almost a ghost town. It sat deserted and forlorn, left to die on the arid acres, a bleached steer carcass on a sandy desert. Sagebrush rolled across the parched fields as jack rabbits run on the plains of Kansas, unobstructed by the abandoned buildings. Even many of these structures were destroyed by "mysterious" fires.

The town didn't die a total death or pass into obscurity because along came former resident, Cornelius "Ed "Pope. Ed's roots are in Allensworth. He lived there as a young boy, for an important three years of his life, from nineteen thirty-eight through nineteen forty. "The thing I loved the most about Allensworth was the school," he fondly recalls. "My parents were migrant farm workers so I couldn't attend school regularly much of the time because we moved too often. When I did get to an occasional school I was cursed and beaten by the white children and scorned by the teachers. Here I didn't have to fight to go to school and learning was a pleasure." *(Are you listening Colonel Allensworth?)*

When he realized what was happening to the disappearing town he loved, Ed decided he couldn't just stand by and watch it vanish entirely. He knew the profound significance it could mean to Afro-Americans. As an employee for the State Department of

Parks and Recreation he saw a way to revive the town: to give it an honorary status. Since 1969, Ed, (now retired) and a growing number of civic minded "Friends of Allensworth" have been spending great amounts of time and money restoring the buildings and surroundings.

On October 9, 1976 the town of Allensworth regained status and recognition when it was designated the Col. Allensworth State Park, the only Black national heritage park in California. It is also the only California town to be founded and governed solely by Afro-Americans. It fostered the first Black Justice of the Peace and the first Black constable in the State. Today restorations include the library, general store, a shady park and the house where the Allensworth family lived, with more soon to come.

The heart of the town seemed to die with Col. Allensworth but its soul and spirit live on. Revitalized by love of citizens and friends, and visited by thousands each year, the park will stand, a monument to the spirit of a valiant, illustrious and principled man. And the world will know that there once was this noble Black man who triumphed over life's obstacles enough to leave behind a rich legacy to the history of his race.

The Schoolhouse

The Library, one of the first buildings erected in the town of Allensworth. It is being re-stocked by Friends of Allensworth.

APPENDIX I

(Partial text of Allensworth's lectures, the *Battle of Life and How to Fight It* and *The Five Manly Virtues* combined as in newspaper accounts. Appended because it shows the magnanimity of Allensworth's character and philosophy and has much that can pertain to today's world).

"There is a bright side to life, and a heroic and noble side to human nature, as exemplified in the lives of many men and women who have conquered in the battle of life. These inspire us with noble ideals, and prove by their example the possible fruitage of human endeavor. Of such class, Benjamin Franklin stands almost alone in his ability to overcome adverse circumstances, and while such heroism is not, and probably never will be, an every day occurrence, rightly studied, every life should serve as an impetus to those who 'having eyes see not' the satisfaction in store for all that equip themselves properly for the duties and responsibilities of life.

"In considering the characters that have made history it is interesting to note that a large per cent of them were cradled in obscurity, and attained a notable place on the world's roll of honor only by refusing to acknowledge environment {as} master of their destiny: The father of Columbus was a weaver; of Homer, a farmer; of Demosthenes, a cutter; of Virgil, a porter; and of Franklin, a soap boiler. . .

"From the first inception of this great nation, industry was the vital spark, the embryonic promise of its future glory. The Pilgrim Fathers in their quest for civil and religious freedom planted on Plymouth Rock the habits of industry, which, as the generations passed, became so thrifty and fruitful that 'all have got the seed'.

"It was impossible to separate from the Puritan character the quality of industry. It was interwoven with his religion, his love of freedom and his frugality. It stood him well in hand during the days of monarchial oppression, when George the Third issued his arbitrary command that the Colonists should work no more in wood and iron; when his soldiery patrolled our forests, marking as the 'Kings own' our giant sentinels. Thank God there was no abatement of their infant industries until the call to arms; and today this scorned command is answered from ocean to ocean, from the Great Lakes to the Great Gulf, in the shrieking of ten thousand engines; in the whirl of burnished steel, in the ceaseless turning of innumerable wheels.

"Consider in a wider and a more general scope what industry has done: It has built the Pyramids on Egypt's plains; erected the gorgeous Temple of Jerusalem; reared the Seven Hilled City, scaled the stormy, cloud-capped Alps, and tunneled their interior; leveled the forest of a New World, and reared in their stead a community of States and Nations. It has brought from the marble block the exquisite creations of genius; it has put in motion millions of spindles; harnessed as many iron steeds to as many freight cars and sent them flying from village to city, from nation to nation; it has tunneled mountains of granite, and annihilated space with the lightning's speed; it has whitened the waters of the world with the sails of a hundred nations; navigated every sea, and explored every land. It has reduced Nature in its thousands of forms to as many sciences; taught her laws; prophesied her future movements; measured her untrodden spaces, counted her myriad hosts of worlds and computed their distances, dimensions and velocities.

"All of these wonderful things and more it has accomplished in the physical world, the conception of which in their entirety would have been impossible in our fathers' time, and yet monuments of constructive genius are not to be compared with the living domes of intellectuality, sparkling temples of virtue, and the rich glory-wreathed sanctuaries of religion which industry has wrought from the minds of men. The most potent forces of life are those which are silent and unseen,— whose subtle workings are the concomitants of that mysterious mechanism that belongs to the boundless and indefinable realms of thought. The toil-sweated productions of wealth, piled in vast profusion around a Rothschild or Rockefeller are nothing when weighed against the stores of wisdom, the treasuries of knowledge, and the strength, beauty and glory with which this victorious virtue has enriched and adorned a great multitude of minds during the march of a hundred generations.

"The industry of Newton, Howard and Channing means much to us who have profited by the months and years of earnest effort employed by them to make the world better for their having lived in it.

"Those who have engaged in the battle of life should be sure that the cause in which they have enlisted is a good one,—one that God and Nature sanction—and then they would be true to it and fight for it. The victory is to the strong, and to those who throw mind, heart and soul into an undertaking, not considering the results so much as the accomplishment of today's duty.

"If you would win friends, be steady and true to yourself. Be the unfailing friend of your own purpose; stand by your own character and others will come to your aid. Though your ideal of today appears far removed, it is well to reflect that every step takes you nearer to it.

"So closely are industry and fidelity united that the one is ever associated in our minds with the other, though fidelity does not necessarily suggest the degree of activity that industry presupposes. Both qualities may be cultivated to an extent such as to round out the character and make man master of himself, though I believe that at birth the virtues exist in embryo and that in some way they are much more strongly marked than in others. For this reason life is a far greater struggle for some than for others, and those who have worked industriously to cultivate these qualities often succeed in eclipsing those to whom Nature was much kinder.

"Gentleness, the virtue which softens and gives amiability to our disposition and behavior, is possibly more potent in its objective influence than any of the virtues, though we would by no means confuse this characteristic with a passive tameness of spirit that is suggestive of indifference and absence of character. Conformity is not gentleness but weakness. Gentleness presupposes intelligence and sympathy, hence in order to aid in bringing about proper conditions, the gentlest person may often appear to the ignorant and unthinking as cruel and kind.

"True gentleness, therefore is to be carefully distinguished from the mean spirits of cowards, and the fawning assent of sycophants; it renounces no just right from fear; it gives up no important truth from flattery; it is indeed, not only consistent with a firm mind, but it necessarily requires a manly spirit and a fixed principle in order to give it any real value. It stands opposed to harshness and severity, to pride and arrogance, to violence and oppression.

"Added to the virtues already expanded, in order to become equipped for the combat of life, one must possess fortitude in no small degree. I have thought that if the battle is not always to the strong, the victory is often his who has learned to bear the vicissitudes of the strife with hope and patience.

"Though fortitude and courage are generally considered as identical in meaning, there is a distinct difference between these leading manly characteristics. Courage resists danger; fortitude supports pain. Courage may be a virtue or a vice, according to the controlling circumstances; fortitude is always a virtue,—we speak of a desperate courage, but not of a desperate fortitude.

"Fortitude is strongest in those who have endured most. The skilled mariner obtains his best experience amid storms and tempests, thus augmenting his self-reliance and courage and learning the highest discipline. So from the storms of life, from its rude shocks of misfortune and its blasts of adversity does man become strong, courageous and victorious.

"In order to succeed one must possess in addition to the four virtues named, a goodly amount of Prudence, or, in other words, a knowledge of what is to be desired and avoided, else failure may be expected. A wise discrimination as to choice both of ends and means, and the power of suiting words and actions with reference to controlling circumstances are indispensable to one who engages in the battle of life; provided time is utilized to a purpose.

"While it is true that human nature is moulded by a thousand subtle influences—environment, precept, education, literature and precedent, man must ever be the active agent of his own well being and doing. This is well illustrated by the works of scientific men in the caution with which they present their ideas. Though the science of today is in many respects as absolute as mathematics, yet they who have delved to the greatest depths recognize the vast treasuries of knowledge that lie beyond the grasp of even the wisest, and they realize that we are still compelled to reason from relative premises. In the moral world, however, there is no occasion for humility, since man may be an arbiter of his own fate, and in the degree that he depends upon outside influences to do for him what he is capable of doing for himself, he is guilty of weakness such as to preclude the possibility of growth. One must learn to govern self before attempting to direct or govern others, otherwise his influence is of little value. The superficiality of self-constituted leadership is acknowledged by all classes of people, yet comparatively few recognize the principle that underlies its weakness.

Though wealth and position may not be the inheritance of all, provided one is capable of conceiving of true character, there is nothing to interfere with one's possession of it, nor any excuse for the weak links in the chain. In most cases they are there—this cannot be gainsaid—but only because one is unwilling to "sell all" that he has in order to secure it. What we care for most, we get. If one is willing to subordinate every other faculty to the acquisition of wealth, he may get wealth; if to knowledge, he may acquire it. And if one desires above all else to possess the five manly virtues—or character—it may be his in abundance.

"When the shadows of earth are passing away and the realities of another life shall dawn, I fear there are many so-called victors who will take inferior positions, since the time has come when true worth alone will pass muster. Sometimes in vision I see the great ones of earth putting in their claims for recognition: The orator challenged, pleads past eloquence that has swayed thousands like corn in the summer wind; moved them to tears and incited them to passion; the poet urges his claim, in that he brought people to tears through his songs of love; the painter begs for recognition because of his careful reproduction of Nature and its influence in lifting up, and civilizing, his fellow men; the sculptor boasts of his ability to give speech to marble and breath to plastic clay. Last of all the warrior begs consideration in that though he has planned mighty battles, slain thousands, caused kings and empires to tremble at his will, all was done in the cause of mercy to prevent a fiercer struggle and a bloodier carnage.

"Still in a dream I see them all pass on to great and sure reward, each having improved his talent and fulfilled his duty according to the light given. And yet the vision is incomplete—I marvel that the richest diadems are reserved for these, when suddenly a great and surging throng are thrown on canvas! They are without scepter or laurel wreath, the purple or ermine of kings; I recognize no Demosthenes, Homer, Michael Angelo nor Napoleon, but challenged, I hear a weak response: "I have loved and cared for little children"; and another, "I have visited the sick and imprisoned, and offered the cup of cold water in His name".

"All life is a battle, and every man has his decisive one. We all have our moral Marengos and Waterloos, where we win or lose the crown of victory. A "yes" or "no" has cost many a man his fortune and has revealed limitations that even the possessor did not dream existed. It is well that a few simple rules of moral welfare should be remembered when decisive conflicts are imminent:

"1. Never place on guard a doubtful principle. Your sentinel will be sure to betray you.

"2. Never change your position in the face of an enemy. This was a fatal policy to Russians at Austerlitz; it has caused many a disgraceful defeat in moral and spiritual warfare.

"3. Never abandon the high ground of right for the low lands and swamps of expedience. No man was ever lost in a straight road.

"4. Never yield an inch to the enemy. It is hard to recover a line that has begun to retreat.

"It appears to be the natural desire of every human heart to live to a great age, and yet a large per cent exist without purpose, and can give no logical reason for desiring it to be extended.

Unrest and dissatisfaction are on every hand, and the question as to the utility or value of life is uppermost with the majority. There is a practical solution of life in the minds of nearly all thinking people, which could become effective if there were less incredulity existing among those who long for humane and proper conditions. They recognize wrong and selfishness, but believe it to be inevitable, and therefore make no effort to surmount precedent. If we put on the armor of the five virtues and wear it with credit, we can by example alone overcome much of the skepticism that exists concerning the possibilities of human nature strength and stability. There is much latent force both in men and women of which the world knows nothing, simply because the conditions of their lives are such that their strongest gifts remain dormant. It is questionable whether even the noblest and best have a full comprehension of their own heroism. For instance, in the case recently quoted of an obscure laboring man meeting death while closing a switch, the failure to do which would have cost the lives of a large number of people,—in all probability this was the outgrowth of kindness and brotherly love, the depth of which the man was not conscious until put to the test. And yet, 'Greater love hath no man than this, that a man lay down his life for his friend' (*John 15:13*)

"That which raises a country; that which strengthens it; that which spreads its power and creates its moral influence is character! And of this we can all be possessed.

" 'This above all, to thine own self be true; and it must follow as the night the day, thou canst not then be false to any man'. " (*Shakespeare: Hamlet, Act I, Scene 3*).

APPENDIX II

(Continuation of the text of paper by Allensworth concerning his views of *"Social Status and Race"* printed in the *New York Age.*

"Our people are educated by our leaders, by men who are selected for places of trust and honor; men who are supposed to voice our sentiments; men whose social and finanacial standing among us are supposed to be equal to that of those who occupy similar positions of leadership among white men but too often they betray us by conduct that scandalizes the race. We do not realize, as fully as we should, that we hold to many false ideas and practices in social life, that militate against us more than any other sociological factor. We have among us as leaders, men who feast and fatten upon our credulity and generosity. Some of the most vicious of the country are our reputed leaders. We have no rigid rule of exclusion by which our homes and families may be protected against the incursions of fat indolents and dangerous libertines; our social condidion must be greatly improved before any such rule will ever be generally en-forced or observed. We must keep the education of the home up to that of the school house, that we may be able to enforce at home the rules of decency and morality, the laws of pure and safe homes the world over.

"This is done in some homes, but at the expense of being charged with being 'stuck up and trying to get away from the race'. We have some, but we need more, leaders, who will encourage the people to draw around their homes a rigid line against the intrusion of dissolute and scandalous persons who impose themselves up on us, and declare that one colored man is 'just as good as another'.

"We should refute the white man's slander, 'all colored people are alike'. The public is affected by the tendency to ignore the leadership of our deserving and safe professional men, men who by education and position should be accepted as leaders. These professional men who are entitled to leadership are too often forced aside by certain ministers, who are fitted neither by nature nor by training for such work. It makes no difference with what immorality some of our ministerial leaders may be charged, he is still retained in the pulpit and allowed to lead, even when the charge is proved. What effect can such leadership have upon the morals of our people?

"Yet when our professional men of Christian culture and refinement fail to unite with our churches, with such officials and pastors with less knowledge of the Bible than an ordinary Sunday School pupil, we charge them with trying to get away from the race. We must improve our social status, we must have social distinctions; we must draw a line between the refined and unrefined. Jesus drew the line and had His intimate social friends and why not we?".

APPENDIX III

Transcriptions of a few of the letters to President Grover Cleveland, the War Department and others from friends of Allensworth (1884 to 1886) recommending his appointment as Chaplain 1884 to 1886.

• "To the President: I desire, and most heartily, to commend him {Allensworth} to your favorable consideration. I have known him for many years, and have at all times found him faithful and conservative; in the discharge of all duties imposed upon him prompt, intelligent and true. I should be gratified, indeed, to know that you had honored and trusted a man so deserving."

—Signed Hon. John O. Hodges, Supt. of City Schools, Lexington, Ky. and Editor of the Lexington Observer.

• "To President Cleveland: Mr. Allensworth is a minister in good standing in the Baptist Church, an ex slave who has overcome all the obstacles of that unfortunate class of our fellow citizens, and made himself by self culture and force of character a man respected by all who know him. We gladly endorse his application for such an appointment, and feel that it is a fit one to be made."

— Mssrs. Emmett G. Logan and E. Polk Johnson, Editors of the Louisville Times

• "I am well acquainted with the Rev. Allen Allensworth, an ex-slave, who by his own exertions and natural ability has arisen to high standing as a Baptist Minister. He lived near me, and was pastor of the principal Baptist Church in Southern Kentucky for many years, and I can attest to his good character and ministerial attainments. He is competent and worthy; his appointment would give satisfaction to all who are acquainted with him."

— Ex. Lt. Governor Underwood.

• "It is with pleasure that I join in with others in recommending and requesting the appointment of Rev. Allen Allensworth as Chaplain in a regiment of colored troops in the U.S. Army, who was once a slave in our family, and since his freedom has obtained and kept the respect of all who know him."

—Mr. W.N. Bayliss, son-in-law of first owner, A.P. Starbird.

This letter is endorsed by Mrs. A.P. Starbird (Miss Bett as she was known to the young slave).

• "It gives me pleasure to add to the numerous testimonials of Rev. Allen Allensworth that which I know of this valuable man. Having been a teacher under me for some time I was so associated with him that I could not but be informed as to his worth, as a teacher, and to his race in general. He possesses in high degree all those characteristics and embellishments which belong to the succesful teacher. He possesses a power for good over the colored race that is trully remarkable and commands the respect of all who are so furtunate as to know him. He will accomplish good for his race in whatever field or capacity he may work for them. I most heartily recommend him to any position in which he is to be intrusted with the interest of the colored race under the Government of the United States."
—Prof. W.B. Wylie, Supt. of Graded Schools, Bowling Green, Ky.

• "To the Honorable Sec'y of War.
Sir:
I beg to recommend to your most favorable consideration Rev. Allen Allensworth for the position of Chaplain in the 24th Regiment of Infantry, colored—the Commission for the present Officer being about to expire by limitation.

Mr. Allensworth and I were boys together and his mother was in my employ for many years as Cook, another son being my dining room servant, and I have consequently had abundant opportunity to learn all about them.

Afterwards, while Mayor of Louisville, I came frequently in contact with Mr. Allen Allensworth and watched his course with his people with great interest and pleasure.

His every utterance was dignified and manly, and his entire effort was to preserve the proper and kindly relations between the Races.

He is a comparatively young man, being about 43 years old, very intelligent and active in his duties and would be a faithful and creditable official. I should esteem it a very great favor if he could be successful in his aspirations.

I have had a conversation with His Excellency the President and it is at his suggestion that this letter has been written."

With Great respect

Very truly yours

S/Charles D. Jacob

BIBLIOGRAPHY

Alexander, Charles, *Battles and Victories of Allen Allensworth*,
Sherman French & Co. Boston, 1914 (Out of Print)

Beasley, Delilah; *The Negro Trail Blazers*; 1919, Los Angeles
Reprinted, R & E, Saratoga Calif. 1968.

Brown, William Wells, *The Negro in the American Rebellion*,
1867, Reprinted by Citadel Press, New York, 1971

Claflin, Edward Beecher; *Sojourner Truth and the Struggle
for Freedom,* Barron's Educational Series, Inc. 1987 New York

Clark, Michael James Tinsley, *A History of the Twenty Fourth
U.S. Infantry Regiment in Utah,* 1896 -1980 (diss.) University of Utah 1979

David, Jan and Elaine Crane; *The Black Soldier, From the
American Revolution to Viet Nam*; William Morrow, 1971

Fadiman, Clifton, *The American Treasury,* Curtis Publishing

Fowler, Arlen, *The Black Infantry in the West*, Greenwood
Publishing, Westport, Conn

Federal Writers Project for the W.P.A., California, *A Guide to
the Golden State*

Friedel, Frank, *The Splendid Little War,* Bramhall House
division of Clarkson Potter/ Little Brown 1958

Furnas, J.C. *Goodbye to Uncle Tom,* William Sloane Associates,
New York, 1956

Hughes, Langston; *A Pictorial History of the Negro in America,
1902 to 1967* (Republished 1983, Crown Publishers),

Levinson, Dorothy; *The Reconstruction;* Franklin Watts; 1970

Lomax, Louis E.;*The Negro Revolt;* Harper Bros, New York, 1962

McFeely, William S. *Frederick Douglass*; Simon and
Schuster, New York, 1991

Morison, Samuel Eliot; Commager, Henry Steele; Leuchtenburg, William E. A *Concise History of the American Republic*, Oxford University Press, New York 1977

Murray, Lindley; *English Reader, Horatio Hill & Co. Concord New Hampshire 1828*

Phillips, Ulrich Bonnell; *American Negro Slavery*, D. Appleton & Co. New York, 1918

Porter, Ebenezer; *Rhetorical Reader*; Mark H. Newman Publisher (220th edition 1835)

Scipio, L. Albert II; *The Last of the Black Regulars;* Roman Publisher, Silver Spring, Md. 1983

Simmons,William J., *Men of Mark, Eminent, Progressive and Rising;* Arno Publications, New York, 1887

Smock, Raymond and Harlan, Louis; *The Booker T. Washington Papers, Vol. 13;* 1914 -15; University of Illinois Press, Chicago, 1984.

U.S. Army Historical Research Collection: *History of Negro Soldiers in the Spanish American War*, by Edward Johnson, 1899

U.S.Army Chaplaincy; 1865 - 1920 *Up From Handyman*

Steward, Rev. T.G., *Active Service: or Religious Work Among U.S. Soldiers,* National Archives.

FOOTNOTES

1) Catherine Drinker Bowen, *Biography: The Craft and the Call ing* (Little Brown and Company, Boston, MA, 1969) page 49

2) Recorded in a Federal Writers' Project book, *Lay My Burden Down*, University of Chicago Press. 1945 (page 126)

3) Charles Alelxander, *Battles and Victories of Allen Allensworth,* (Boston, MA . Sherman French & Company, 1914) All quotes not attributed are from this book.

4) Lindley Murray, *English Reader*, Concord, New Hampshire, 1828, Horatio Hill & Co., page 13.

5) Clifton Fadiman, Ed., *The American Treasury*, 1455-1955, New York, Harper & Brothers, 1955, page 374

6) Ibid, page 379

7) Morison, Commager and Leuchtenburg, *Concise History of the American Republic,* Oxford University Press, New York, 1977; page 329

8) Beasley, Delilah, *The Negro Trail-Blazers of California*, 1919, reprinted 1968 by R & E Publishers, Saratoga California.(now out of print).